D1125851

BACK TO
BREMEN

Enjoy the read!
Cecelia
Wilson

Hope you like
the Book,
Edith

BACK TO
BREMEN

THE INSPIRING TRUE STORY OF ONE MOTHER'S JOURNEY TO SAVE HER
CHILDREN THROUGH THE WAR-TORN RUINS OF THE THIRD REICH.

CECELIA
WILSON

MEATH

OGHMA CREATIVE MEDIA

www.oghmacreative.com

Books from Meath Press and Oghma Creative Media may be purchased educational, business, or sales promotional use. For information, please e-mail the Admin Department at venessa@ oghmacreative.net.

ISBN: 978-1-63373-263-6

Interior Design by Casey W. Cowan
Editing by Michael L. Frizell

Meath Press
Oghma Creative Media
Bentonville, Arkansas
www.oghmacreative.com

To my three great loves:
Dennis, Cody, and Cheyenne

and

to Edith,
Thank you for long talks, laughter,
Dr. Peppers, and popcorn

For Edith...

...and in memory of Marta, whose eyes grace the cover of this book.

CONTENTS

"…but the donkey, seeing that no good wind was blowing, ran away and set out on the road to Bremen."

—The Town Musicians of Bremen, The Brothers Grimm

ONE
THE END OF THE ROAD
MAY 1945

Karl-Heinz and I became true partners in crime that day.

I was nine, Karl-Heinz had just turned twelve, and we were both old enough to know we would be in trouble. Marta Röpke was not a large woman and she had never been the disciplinarian in our family, but the war had forged in our mother a steely resolve to see that her family was kept intact. She had preached *"always stay together"* to all of us so often that it was imprinted in our minds. And keeping seven children together during the length of the war without the help of my oldest brother, Günter, and my father, Diedrech, had been quite a task.

Much of the village we entered had recently sustained heavy damage, but the shops that had been able to withstand the worst of the bombings were open for business, providing services and sparse goods to the locals, and accepting almost any form of payment offered.

"Edith!" my brother whispered as loudly as possible to get my attention. He cut his eyes toward the small shop up the street from where we stood.

I nodded. He didn't have to say anything more; my nose told me all I needed to know. We had just located a bakery, and as the scent of warm bread floated on the morning breeze toward us, my mouth watered. For two German children who had eaten nothing but stolen vegetables for weeks, we were desperate to taste what had been tempting our senses and making our empty stomachs groan all morning.

The Second World War had ended in Europe and Hitler was dead. But, we could not feel relief. Germany was in shambles and our only thought was returning home to Bremen in the northwest. For two months we hiked with Frau Meier, her son, and two German soldiers from eastern Germany after escaping from the Soviets. We were now somewhere in British-occupied western Germany, but the road seemed to stretch to infinity.

And while the twelve of us had walked together for hundreds of miles, we were hardly alone. Every day, we were surrounded by thousands of souls who, like us, were just trying to get home, yet none us were sure what we would find when we reached our destinations. The longer we walked, the more the refugees seemed to increase exponentially, and the seemingly endless sea of humanity appeared dazed, shocked, and bitterly tired of the war that had brought so much death and destruction.

There was no doubt the crowds included criminals, spies, and Nazi officers trying to avoid detection, and Mother warned us of those dangers often. Despite knowing the repercussions we would endure once our mother saw us again, hunger drove us closer to the open doors of the bakery that was now only steps away.

My heart beat loudly as we approached the front of the shop. Through the window I could see breads and pastries, and I thought I might reel at the sight. I could also see my reflection and was mortified. I hadn't seen myself for almost two months, and I winced, wishing I could forget the image. None of us had bathed, washed our clothes, brushed our teeth, or combed our hair. I have no doubt we smelled terrible. My shoes were in poor condition: they remained either soaked from rain, or dried and cracked from wear and tear. My feet ached from trudging through fields, up hills and across dirt and gravel. The filthy, tattered clothes I wore were all I owned now and they literally hung off of my increasingly shrinking frame. But that was no surprise; we never knew when or from where our next meal would come. We had sipped water from streams we spied along the way or, after a rain shower, we even resorted to finding puddles in order to quench our thirst. And none of us had eaten anything beyond what little we could find near roads or in pastures.

I felt sorry for the farmers whose properties we had passed through. Their hard labor suffered from all the foot traffic in those months at the end of the war. Like us, many people avoided the more-traveled roads to get home. Like thousands of others near starvation, we were driven to steal cabbage, potatoes, and any other vegetables or fruits we could find in tilled ground and orchards. When a garden was spotted, there would be a rush of people digging up what could be found before the owner spotted us. Grabbing a carrot, we would break off the green tops and use the leafy stems as brushes to clean off as much dirt as possible from our stolen entrée before eating it raw.

Famished and exhausted, we woke in the wooded countryside to the intoxicating aroma of homemade bread floating from the village's center. Slipping away from our mother's ever-watchful eye, Karl-Heinz and I had stealthily followed the scent until we had located the bakery.

Knowing we looked like vagabonds, I was hesitant to enter the shop, but Karl-Heinz elbowed me in the side and we stumbled through the entry at the same time. Inside, was an elderly man on the other side of a counter, waiting on patrons willing to buy or barter for his baked goods. We made a feeble attempt to blend in, pretending to nonchalantly peer at the food on display on the shelves inside the glass counter, but it was painfully obvious we were without ration cards or Reich marks and everyone in that shop knew it. No doubt, the man was watching the two wretched-looking children in his shop, suspicious of our motives as we loitered behind his legitimate customers.

I glanced over at Karl-Heinz and realized he was not focused on what was inside the counter, but what was displayed *on* the counter: several long, plump loaves of golden brown bread stacked one atop the other. He didn't have to look at me to communicate his thoughts. It was if his eyes had tracers telegraphing his objective. The only question now was when the timing was right to follow through on the plan.

There was a *hausfrau* speaking to the elderly baker, and though I could see her mouth forming the words, all I could hear was my own heavy breathing. I swallowed and was sure the seven or eight men and women in the shop could hear the sound as it traveled down my throat. My parents would be mortified. They had not raised any of us to steal, but here my brother and I stood, contemplating just that. I looked up and was sure my thoughts were being read. I noticed the baker was torn between watching us and focusing on the *hausfrau's* requests. She pointed to some item she wanted on a lower shelf and as the old baker leaned over to pick it up, Karl-Heinz made his move, snatching three loaves of bread in quick order, elbowing his way through the startled patrons, and sprinting for the door. I followed suit, grabbing a pair of loaves and running like mad in my brother's wake.

We darted from the bakery and headed down the street as quickly as our legs could carry us, but it didn't take the baker long to chase after us. His face was red as he hobbled out of the shop, yelling for us—the thieves—to stop immediately, *"Diebe! Halten Sie sofort!"*

My legs were burning and my side hurt, but I continued to follow Karl-Heinz down the street and around a building with our arms loaded with the spoils of our campaign. And we kept running, even though we were well out of sight of the blustering baker who had long since run out of steam and given up the chase with a string of expletives.

As we reached the outskirts of the village, we finally felt comfortable enough to slow our pace. We felt winded but jubilant, and couldn't wait to share our morning's work with our family. Within ten minutes or so we had reached the woods where we had spent the night and our two older sisters, Helga and Elfriede, ran to meet us.

"Where have you two been?" Elfriede asked as she fell into step beside us.

Karl-Heinz smiled smugly, lifting his arms to better showcase the bread as the rest of our traveling companions came into view among the trees ahead, "Getting food."

"Hmm. You didn't find *that* in the woods," our oldest sister Helga grinned, eyeing the bread with appreciation. "You two do realize you could have been caught." It was more a statement than a question.

Though I rarely talked back to Helga, I was feeling rather confident for once. "We could have been, but we were faster."

By the time we reached the tree line, Elfriede had taken off her coat and spread it on the ground. Karl-Heinz and I dropped to our knees and placed the loaves on the makeshift "tablecloth" while our younger sisters, Waltraut and Inge, circled us, delighted at the sight of their next meal. Helga and Elfriede began tearing the loaves into manageable portions to share with our group as Frau Meier and her son Hans sat down beside them. The two German soldiers joined the others, and we were soon peppered with questions which we answered with gusto, proud they were all excited to hear about our morning expedition. All, that is, but our mother.

By now, Karl-Heinz was almost as tall as she was, but when she was angry, she seemed to tower above us. And there was little doubt at the moment she was angry. With arms crossed and fluent German searing our ears, she scolded us furiously, reminding us of the real danger we had been in. "You know we must all stay together. You could have gotten lost or kidnapped or killed. Don't ever do that again!"

At that exact moment, our youngest sibling, four-year-old Egon, squeezed his way between the onlookers. Immediately, he pinched off a helping of bread, stuffed it in his mouth, and proclaimed it delicious.

"Lecker!"

It was enough to break the tension. Mother couldn't help but laugh, and though we had been chastised, we were, at least, forgiven. A portion of the bread, to be saved for later, was wrapped in a scarf Frau Meier had been wearing, but the remainder was passed around and eaten slowly, languidly. Karl-Heinz and I accepted our shares, relishing the taste that had haunted us since we had first opened our eyes that day.

Our little adventure was over. We had the admiration of our siblings for bringing back a satisfying meal, and had, fortunately, not gotten caught. But we were also children with years of firsthand knowledge that lives hang in the balance over much lesser offenses than stealing. So, despite our "heroic" activities on behalf of our family that day, Karl-Heinz and I heeded our mother's admonition and never again considered such risky behavior.

On the open roads in Germany at the end of the war, there was little electricity, few radios, and certainly no televisions, cell phones, or Twitter. News was passed along in the form of rumors and hushed conversations. We had already been told that Hitler had killed himself, but word was now spreading that Goebbels, the Propaganda Minister, and his wife had committed suicide as well, just after killing their six children. As always, mother warned all of us not to talk of it. Since the late 30s, mother had taught us incessantly not to discuss matters that dealt with the Nazis. "Keep your eyes down. Stay together. Be very quiet." Mother didn't have to repeat those words, I knew them by heart and so did every one of my siblings. I half-understood it as a younger child, but as I got older I realized the fear that most German citizens had of their neighbors. Who could you trust? Neighbors turned in their neighbors to the Gestapo for "offenses"— whether major, minor, or non-existent—against the Nazis in order to get more ration cards or find employment, and the people they exposed were either harassed by the secret police or totally disappeared as a result.

Even on the open road, being cautious and distrustful was a hard habit to break. While the Third Reich had been destroyed, we weren't sure what the Allies would do now that they were in Germany. We felt safer under British or American control than Soviet, but it had been ingrained in us long ago to remain mute. We had lived under stifled conditions my entire childhood. We could continue to do so until we learned our fate and the fate of our country.

As we neared Hannover, home to the German soldiers traveling with us, we parted ways with the men, knowing the Röpke and Meier families were on our own from that point onward. We had been told there was limited rail service available to Bremen and were all relieved. It was sure to be packed, but I prayed we would all be able to get a seat on the train. Crowded or not, after having walked for so long, sitting in a train car sounded heavenly.

As we made our way to the station, Helga or Elfriede took turns pushing one of our youngest siblings—five-year-old Inge or four-year-old Egon—in the single baby stroller Mother had insisted on bringing along for the trip home. That stroller had been a blessing! Not only did it help the youngsters keep pace with the rest of us, it also gave us relief from having to carry the two little ones. It was, though, a sad statement that the stroller was the only material possession our family had left. Weeks before, one of the wheels had broken off, making pushing the three-wheeled carrier more an exercise in balancing than strolling. There were certainly no stores open along the way to buy parts or repair the damaged stroller.

We arrived at the train station in Hannover and, after a long wait, were finally able to catch a train to Bremen. Mother and Frau Meier ushered all of us onto the train where we managed to find seats together in one of the packed cars. No one checked tickets; none were needed. Those formalities weren't followed during the fresh post-war days. It was more vital to move travelers on to their destinations than worry about who had passage. I watched the countryside slide by as the train moved forward, and the scenery was numbing. It seemed nothing was left unscathed by the war. Bridges and houses were damaged, some were reduced to fragments scattered on the ground; the land even looked battle-weary with trees stripped bare and lifeless, and the earth was battered with potholes, craters and ruts. Bone-tired, I must have dozed for most of the hour or so ride because, before I realized it, I heard Helga talking to Mother, pointing ahead to what must be Bremen.

I sat up, groggy from sleep, anxious to get a look at my beloved hometown. I was stunned; we were all stunned. The city was unrecognizable. Everywhere I looked, I saw heaps of rubble with a bombed-out building's wall rising up from the ashes here and the gutted shell of another structure standing there. What window frames remained intact, were glassless. Once pristine boulevards were littered with brick and mortar, and a fine layer of dust was plastered to everything that still stood upright. What must have been neighborhoods were strewn with stone where homes had once been. But since there were no signs to mark the streets where houses and buildings once stood, and there were few recognizable landmarks, it was difficult to determine which part of the city we were in.

Mother had told us to expect changes in the time we had been gone, but I don't think any of us were expecting what we saw. Since 1940, our family home had been hit three times and my mother had it repaired at least twice. After we were forced to evacuate eastward to Krumhermsdorf, Saxony, in 1943, Mother had her worst fears confirmed: word had come that our house in Bremen had been completely destroyed. As painful as that had been to hear, Mother had thanked God that her children were safe and she reminded us that our lives mattered more than the place we had called "home."

"Where will we go, Mutti?" I asked Mother as I stared at the scarred landscape outside the train's window.

The train began to slow for the approach to the station, but Mother continued to look beyond our heads at the devastation that was Bremen. "I own your grandparents' house now. After we get off the train, I will try to get information on how it fared," she said with as much calm conviction as possible to prevent us from worrying.

Although Mother may have shared her thoughts with the oldest children, Helga, Elfriede, and Karl-Heinz, she didn't let the rest of us know what worried her as we arrived home. With the knowledge that our house had been destroyed, she had pinned her hopes on her late parents' home being intact. If it still stood, we would all have a place to rest our heads at night. If it was gone… I'm not sure Mother had another idea in mind. War left too much uncertainty to plan too far in advance.

When the train finally came to a stop at the station amid spewing steam and the long screech of brakes, Mother stepped down to the platform with all of us following closely behind. The train station was, like most buildings left standing in Bremen, far from untouched, but beneath its fractured framework, it was full of passengers who had arrived to an uncertain existence in the city. With no place else to go for the time being, Mother had us all pair up, hold hands and wind our way through the crowd as one. Frau Meier and her son followed. We found enough space in a corner of the battered train station to call ours and sat down on the cool concrete floor to rest.

After we each had been given food and water by Red Cross officials working at the station, Frau Meier and her son left to gather what information they could on any of their relatives who might still be living in the area. Likewise, Mother put Helga and Elfriede in charge of the younger children while she and Karl-Heinz left to see what they could learn about her parents' house. She had little choice in the matter. It would not have been wise to strike out to find our grandparents' house as a group. Walking through the shambles of the city presented a minefield of dangers. There was no running water and no power, but plenty of broken glass, nails, and potential for injury in the chaos beyond the station's doors.

Since our oldest brother Günter wasn't with us, Karl-Heinz took his place as the oldest son and my Mother relied on him often. I know it made him feel needed to take on the role as our mother's male protector, but he was, after all, still a child himself and he had been forced to grow up quickly, as had all of the older children who understood the dangerous, restrictive life we had been living. So, even though I was in dire need of rest, I smiled as I saw my brother's air of self-importance as he followed Mother. They were only leaving us to wait in line at an information booth. There they would provide an address to officials dispensing what facts they could about our destroyed hometown. It wasn't a taxing job, but Karl-Heinz was happy to feel he was contributing in some way during an otherwise helpless situation.

From where we were sitting, we couldn't see how long the line was Mother and Karl-Heinz had been standing in, but we knew it had to be long. There were so many people seeking information about loved ones, housing and anything else they could learn that we knew we would have to wait some time before they returned to us. My younger sister Waltraut and I had been keeping Inge entertained when I looked up a couple of hours later and saw Mother and Karl-Heinz making their way back through the hordes of people inside what was left of the station. Helga went to meet Mother and I could see them talking, their lowered heads close together so they could hear each other over the multitude of voices surrounding them. I didn't know what Mother was saying, but I could certainly see she was upset. My heart sank. I knew she had not gotten good news. Finally, the trio came back to the corner of the station where the rest of our family sat.

Mother looked at us through teary eyes and took a deep breath, "Your Oma and Opa's house is gone." The bombing campaign over Bremen months before had been one of the heaviest the city had sustained during the war. Years later I read that several hours of bombing had left over 1,000 people dead and more than 8,000 buildings destroyed. On this day, Mother had entered the city knowing the house had been hit, but what she had just learned was the damage to the house was beyond repair. It was a blow, but seeing the condition of the city from the train and the station, none of us had been very surprised to hear that our grandparents' house had been demolished.

We were home, the war was over, and the skies were free of enemy aircraft. But we had no idea how long it would be before we could sit at a table and eat a proper meal or lay our heads on a pillow in a regular bed. The Red Cross would work with us to find temporary housing for our large family, but until then we had little choice… like hundreds of others, we spent our first night back home on the hard, concrete floor of the train station.

TWO
AND SO IT BEGAN
1939

I don't remember life before war. In 1939, I was only three years old and, while I was too young to recall most of the day-to-day details from those early years, I have a few memories that are vivid, I suppose, because of their shocking effect on my life. Despite the political events that were swirling around us, my family was living a rather normal, quiet life. We had no idea that our time together in our little corner of the world was about to be disrupted, changing us all forever.

My parents were both from small families born and raised in Bremen, Germany. My maternal grandparents, Ludwig and Anna Marie Dreyer Koelling, had only two children: my uncle Christian and my mother, Marta Helena. My uncle was a self-professed "momma's boy" who never married and, as a result, never lived too far from my grandparents. He and my mother were extremely close and always doted on one another. Though I don't remember Oma and Opa Koelling, my mother and uncle always shared stories about their sense of humor, a trait they passed down to their children. As a result, my mother was easy-going and fun-loving.

An opera lover, she would often take us with her to performances so she could share that deeply personal appreciation of classical music. She loved coffee, she loved eel, she loved life and loved to laugh, and when Mother found something comical, her laughter was infectious. Though the boys, especially Günter, were a little more serious like Father, I'm certain all the girls inherited our light-heartedness from Mother.

If it is true that opposites attract, my own parents would have been living proof of that old adage. My father, Diedrech Heinrich Herman Röpke—my mother called him Dirk—was as stern and formidable as his very formal name. I suppose, though, he came by it naturally. He was an only child whose mother died before she was twenty-eight; his father died the following year. At the age of six, Father was sent to live with his grandparents, only to have them succumb to death when he was ten. Passed from home to home for the remainder of his youth, my father was forced to grow up quickly and become independent much too soon. Perhaps that explained his strict expectations from each of his own children as we were raised.

A tall man with sharp features and piercing eyes, when my father spoke, we listened. It would have been difficult not to hear him since his deep voice seemed to echo off the walls, particularly when he was upset with one of us. The cost for not heeding his word meant we might find ourselves on the wrong end of his leather belt, and that was not something any of us desired. His means of keeping us in line, the tone of his voice, and his stoic demeanor made me almost afraid to be near him for fear I would do something he would not approve of and then I would have to face his wrath. Avoidance seemed easier for me in dealing with my father, but not all my siblings seemed to learn that little pointer. It was certainly a lesson that Helga, who seemed to constantly stay in trouble, might have practiced more often to her benefit. Now that I think about it, I'm not actually sure I ever heard him call her name without it being drawn out in a slow, ominous tone: "Hel-*gaaaa*..."

Many Germans have a love affair with steins and the brews within them, but while Father was a drinker before the war, he didn't do so to excess. He could have been described as steady and dependable. He loved his wife and children and was a hard worker. He made an adequate living through the work of his hands, and he was fortunate to have steady employment at a company where he made furniture. Germany's economy had improved since Hitler became Chancellor and then Führer, but many people had been forced out of their jobs for political reasons. In fact, of fifty-two Jewish stores operating in Bremen in 1938, all were either closed or taken over by "Aryan" operators within a five-month period. Though we were not Jews, we still held our breath with each new law established with ever-increasing ferocity. The Nazis were making their presence felt.

Though they each were accustomed to a small family, my parents decided soon after they married that *they* wanted a large family. Whether they longed for an end to peaceful days or they simply wanted to be in vogue with the ideal German family size at the time, they accomplished their goal. These days when I recount my siblings' births, I laugh and say my parents had their "annual baby." I was their sixth child, born in 1936, and I was followed by younger sisters Waltraut and newborn Inge by August 1939. The final Röpke child, Egon, would appear on the scene later. There were nine of us in all, but my sister Giesela died several months after my birth, just before her third birthday.

Neither of my parents displayed much physical affection toward me or my siblings as we were growing up. We didn't hug or kiss or tell each other, "I love you." Frankly, I'm not sure many people did back then. But Mother, in particular, had a way of letting us know she loved us by showing concern when we were ill, compassion when we were hurt and helping us navigate life's little hurdles with ease. And she always made our house feel like a home.

We lived in a compact, two-story brick house in a modest neighborhood just north of Bremen's city center. Our yard had been framed by a lovely wrought iron fence, but in September 1938, residential iron fences were removed and used as scrap to build tanks and airplanes. Posters in shop windows throughout the city encouraged everyone to help in the effort, but most families we knew were too intimidated *not* to volunteer their fences since those who didn't were looked on with suspicion by the government. Loyalty to Hitler was not to be questioned.

Walking from the front door, visitors to our house would step into a hallway on the main floor. To the right was our living room. I remember an ample beige couch situated against one wall with a small side table perched nearby, a sprinkling of patterned, cushioned chairs positioned around the room, some facing the couch, others facing the window, and there was a massive wooden *schrank*—pronounced shrunk—that stood proudly against the other wall.

Since most rooms in German homes were constructed without built-in closets, a *schrank* provided needed storage for every room. In our living room, the *schrank* had several shelves and drawers that held my mother's silverware, glassware, and china, along with her kitchen linens. Besides being a useful piece of furniture to display or stow items, it was also a beautiful cabinet that Mother kept polished to a high shine. Its sheer size made it the focal point of the room, and Mother was very proud to have friends admire it and comment on her lovely china gleaming from its shelves.

Directly across the hallway from the living room was our kitchen/dining room. The single open room was truly multi-functional. In today's terms, it would certainly be described as open concept. Our table and chairs distinguished one end of the room as the dining area, with the stove and sink defining the other end as the kitchen. On Saturdays, the room also served a third purpose when my father or one of the boys brought in the large, round metal tub from outside and sat it down on the floor near the stove for our once-a-week bath time.

What I recall most about those weekly cleaning sessions was that I wanted to be one of the first to get my turn in that tub. Since water was limited and hot water even more so, it was a lot more enjoyable if I was fortunate enough to be one of the earliest bathers. The problem was, the little ones always got to go first, so the older you were in our family, the less likely your water was warm or fresh. If that wasn't bad enough, as I got older, that tub seemed to shrink with every one of my birthdays.

The only true "bathroom" in the house—minus a tub, of course—was on the upper floor near my parents' bedroom. It boasted a small sink with a larger mirror hanging over it and a commode. That half-bath had very little square footage, but it was one of the most sought-after rooms in the house. A line would form in the mornings outside the bathroom door with the boys constantly complaining that the girls stayed in the room an inordinate amount of time. Since my father was up early getting ready for work and the four oldest children were getting ready for school at the same time, Father was also involved in the morning competition. Of course, he always won the war over bathroom time with one persuasive bark of his booming voice. When he finished and made his way back to his bedroom, the kids' fight for the bathroom began again in earnest.

My parents shared a modest-size bedroom with baby Inge that was located on one end of the second floor. Father, who was a master carpenter, had built their bed and the crib in which Inge slept each night. As a matter of fact, that crib had been passed down from Günter through each successive birth, so it had seen its share of babies. My brothers Günter and Karl-Heinz were given the smallest bedroom in which they shared a bed, and the girls—Helga, Elfriede, Waltraut and I—slept together in the last bedroom in a single large wooden bed, also built by Father. As Inge became older, she, too, would join the sisters in that big bed.

Though it was the norm for my sisters and me to sleep together then, today I certainly can't imagine trying to get a good night's rest with so many people in one bed. Of all the girls, I'm sure Helga felt the brunt of that nightly ritual most keenly. As the oldest girl, only she would have had the luxury of initially having a bed to herself only to have it slowly invaded by more and more girls with each passing year. She didn't exactly take that lying down—no pun intended—and she let us know when we were intruding on her space. I actually remember falling out of bed on more than one occasion, catapulted from the mattress by Helga's pushy elbows and feet! It seemed a long way down to the cold floor from that warm bed, and Helga seldom seemed inclined to help me back up. Father, already tired from a long day at work, would hear me crying and Helga would have to face the consequences for his lack of sleep and my bruised... ego.

We had a single feather comforter that was piled high over the group of girls each night. It was warm, but it was heavy. There were frequent fights over the sheet or the cover, and though our pillow fights might begin as simple fun, they would inevitably end with one girl or another getting hit a little too hard. The injured girl would go running and crying to Father, tattling on the offender. And that offender was almost always Helga. The ruckus in our bedroom was immediately silenced as we heard Father's footsteps nearing our room. Helga's fate was sealed.

Since there were no closets in the bedrooms, each room had its own *schrank*, smaller than the one in the living room, but large enough to hold a small amount of clothes and underclothes for each of us. Just like the crib, outfits were definite hand-me-downs from child to child, but I never minded. It always felt like a new wardrobe had been given to me when I outgrew my old clothes, so I was more than happy to show my friends my "new" dress or shoes. Being the oldest, Günter and Helga wore garments that were much less worn since they either got the newest purchases or the best second-hand clothes from a local shop.

That may explain why Günter was always so fixated on dressing well. As the firstborn (and first son) in our family, he wanted to be just like our father. He had the opportunity to look more mature and more distinguished even at a young age with his "new" clothes, so looking sharp became a habit he relished. It didn't hurt that all the girls in our neighborhood seemed to be enamored of the tall, good looking, neatly dressed young boy with the dark hair and striking blue eyes. He was one of the worst offenders when it came to monopolizing the bathroom and I suspect much of that time was spent grooming in front of the mirror. He was quite the "ladies' man." He would walk girls to school, carry their lunch sacks, and was always winking or grinning at them. They, in return, batted their eyes and practically swooned at his feet. He was the self-declared German Casanova of the primary school!

While the downstairs rooms in our house were more bright and sunny, there were fewer windows upstairs due to the slope of the roof, so little light filtered into the bedrooms. I never really minded that either; I slept much more soundly in a darker room. But, that also meant there was less sunlight to warm the bedrooms when the weather outside grew chilly. Since Bremen is near the North Sea and Denmark, we felt winter's cold acutely. Unfortunately, the only heat for our entire house came from a large potbelly stove that sat in the middle of the kitchen downstairs. Needless to say, the upstairs was considerably colder than the floor below, making our big sister-filled feather bed so cozy that none of us were eager to jump out of it to get ready for the day ahead.

The kitchen was the hub of our home. The round wooden table my father had labored over was large enough to accommodate the entire family, and it took up much of the space in the room. We always ate our meals together as a family, and that table was the center of many daily family discussions. It seemed we were always sitting around that table eating or simply talking, catching up on the day.

The fresh-brewed aroma of coffee was a common scent that drifted through the house in the morning and after our evening meal. Even today, when I smell coffee, I think of my mother. Rationing had been instituted in 1939. Identification and ration cards had been distributed to each household and monthly allotments fixed per person: 700g of meat products, 280g of sugar, dairy products, oils or fats 235g, jelly 100g, .20 liters of milk. Bread, flour, and potatoes could be bought freely, but since coffee was a commodity that was shipped into our country rather than produced locally, it was one of the first items that was difficult to obtain… and my mother loved coffee. She continued to drink what passed for coffee during the shortage, even though she would grimace over the grains used as a substitute for coffee beans.

I remember she had a small coffee grinder attached to a wooden plaque that was nailed to the kitchen wall. The metal grinder was silver and had a lid on top that was opened to place the beans inside. She would manually grind the beans using the handle on front and I would watch through a small glass window as those beans were slowly reduced to a fine dusting of coffee. A little drawer at the bottom of the grinder collected the coffee and was then pulled out to be dumped into a pot. Years later I would see one like it in a movie and I was astonished how excited I was spotting something so seemingly insignificant, yet familiar. Seeing that otherwise-forgotten kitchen utensil flooded my mind with childhood memories.

Learning to cook in that kitchen with all the sisters and Mother inevitably led to one of my Mother's giggling fits.

Once, when the girls were making *apfel kuchen*, Mother pointed at the items laid out on the counter near the sink, "Now, Elfriede, you want to add some cinnamon and sugar to the sliced apples and stir it in well."

Elfriede grabbed a few pinches of each, stirred obediently, and peered up at Mother, "What now, Mutti?"

"Set that aside and we'll make the batter," Mother reached for another bowl. All the girls stood closely together, helping when needed and watching intently as the next set of ingredients was blended together. "Now you'll need two cups of flour."

Anxious to be the first of us to measure it out, Elfriede grabbed a large cup of flour and snatched it away quickly from other outstretched hands just in time to shower us all with a cloud of the white powder. When the dust finally settled, each of our faces was covered with flour and Mother was laughing so hard tears were trickling from her eyes, streaking fine lines down her floured face.

We couldn't help but join in the laughter!

But, it only got worse when we served the *apfel kuchen* after our evening meal. Elfriede was especially proud, claiming most of the credit for making the *kuchen*. She gave some to Father first who took a big bite, chewed for a few seconds, and immediately wrinkled his nose and brow, "What's wrong with the *kuchen*?"

At some point during the cooking lesson, Elfriede had grabbed salt inside of sugar. It made for one briny dessert that few of us wanted to eat. Father was not amused, Elfriede looked like she was about to cry, and Mother dissolved in another round of tear-filled giggles. Before long, the entire kitchen rang with laughter, Elfriede was soon cajoled into joining in, and Father begrudgingly grinned at the madness that had broken out around the table.

One cool September evening in 1939 when we were all, once again, seated around the table, the clattering of utensils and excited banter bouncing off the kitchen walls, a knock was heard on the front door. Normally, we might have missed the sound of someone knocking over the din that surrounded dinner time, but this evening was different. The knock was more forceful, the timing of potential visitors more curious since most of the families in our neighborhood were also sitting down to eat. My parents had not been expecting company.

Father left the kitchen and walked into the hallway to open the front door. When he re-entered the room, he was followed by two uniformed men from the German Army. Their imposing presence filled the room. Sensing the tense air emanating from our parents, we all stopped talking and the room became unusually quiet.

"Please, come in," Mother interjected into the silence. "Would you like anything to eat or drink?"

The men merely shook their heads as they took in the domestic scene in front of them.

Always blunt, my father came quickly to the point. "What may I do for you?" my father asked, his voice tinged with concern.

"You must come with us," one of the two men answered without ceremony. They were both stern, business-like, and seemed to be too pressed for time to provide any other details. The guns at their sides and swastikas on their uniforms impressed upon us all the seriousness of the situation.

I remember glancing at my mother. Normally so composed and collected, she was visibly upset, though I wasn't sure why at the time. "Where are you taking him?" she asked boldly as she rose from the table with baby Inge in her arms.

The men wouldn't say. Instead, they curtly ordered my father to gather his things and leave with them immediately. Father took a quick look around at all of us before he nodded and made his way upstairs to pack while Mother tried her best to appear calm. I could tell my older brothers and sisters were disturbed, which naturally upset me and the younger ones in turn. Before long, one child was whimpering and another was wiping tears. The soldiers stood silent, unwilling to talk, taking in each increasingly sadder face staring back at them. Soon, we were all crying, making the two uniformed men more and more uncomfortable. They shifted from one foot to another, clearing their throats, averting their eyes. Had it not been so serious, it might have been comical, but I knew it was no laughing matter because Mother couldn't even smile.

By the time Father came back downstairs, our cries had become sobs and we only had minutes to say hasty goodbyes. It was then that Father did something he had never done before, reinforcing what we each knew, but had seldom seen. He showed us he loved us. And he proved it that night when he bent to give us each a hug.

His normally stoic demeanor was shaken as he quickly embraced me and all the younger children one at a time. He then turned to face his first-born. Günter was almost ten, but he and my father both understood that the young boy would now be the "man" of the house. The man Günter so wanted to emulate, so wanted to become, was leaving. He tried his best to stop the quivering of his lower lip as he looked up at Father, "Vati, don't go!"

My father didn't speak, but gave Günter a quick, rough hug and left his thoughts unspoken between them.

"Dirk," Mother's voice broke as she searched his face. He gathered her and Inge to him briefly before he picked up his bundle of packed clothes and made a hurried exit. As for the soldiers who led him out of the house, I'm sure they were grateful to be leaving the loud, sad scene behind them.

It happened so quickly that only after the front door slammed shut did I realize my father had not even been allowed to finish his meal. I don't recall how long we cried, but Mother eventually joined in the sorrow and even newborn Inge chimed in with her own wails. Tending to Inge, my mother urged us all to clean our plates, but we were all too upset to do more than pick at the remaining food in front of us.

I didn't know what it all meant, but Mother did her best to explain it in terms that might make sense to her children. What my mother didn't fully comprehend at the time was why her forty-year-old husband was needed in the Germany Army. We didn't know it was just the beginning of dangerous times for us all. The year before, Hitler had annexed Austria; in March 1939, he had taken Czechoslovakia. By September, as we were eating our evening meal, he had invaded Poland, and Britain and France had declared war on Germany. The world trembled in unison with our family. The present was full of fear and in the coming years we would all learn how right we were to have cried for our loved ones.

THREE
THE BRITISH ARE COMING
1940

It was months before we saw Father again. Our first reunion with him occurred when he was traveling through by train and had a short layover in Bremen. Mother told us we could visit him and, after we insisted on taking a gift with us, she agreed we could walk several blocks out of our way to Market Square and buy him a special treat on the way to the train station.

For a large city, Bremen always felt comfortable and welcoming to me and I loved walking to the city center. Its grand Town Hall built in the 1400s and the majestic early Gothic St. Peter's Cathedral with its twin towers soaring upward defined the city's skyline and made me proud of my beautiful birthplace. We walked by the ancient statue of Roland and ducked into my father's favorite pastry shop. The proprietor greeted us when we walked through the door. A stooped, elderly man with white hair and a large mustache, he never failed to make me smile when I saw him.

Mother told him the reason for our hurried visit and he pointed a crooked finger to a freshly made *obst torte*. "Ah, that will make your papa's mouth water!"

Mother laughed in agreement while he wrapped it in paper for the short walk on to the station. She paid him and we all filed out of the old brick building. The bell clinked over the door as we made our exit and I looked back at the old gentleman. He winked at me and I giggled.

The train station was about a ten-minute walk from the city center and the excitement bubbled up inside of me as we got closer. As a child, there were few things as exhilarating as watching the trains pull in and out of the station. The ticket counters were such hubs of activity; there were so many people traveling to so many different destinations. I didn't quite understand how all those people could have so many places to go, but I was fascinated watching it all unfold before me.

Standing on the platform, Karl-Heinz and I watched Father's train lumber its way toward us. "Look, Edith, here comes Vati's train now!" Karl-Heinz yelled above the noise surrounding us.

The engine was massive and when it slowly steamed its way to a stop, Karl-Heinz was standing close enough to the platform's edge that the steam spewing from its brakes thoroughly enveloped him. Within seconds, all I could see was the top of his head. When he reappeared through the fog, he was bent over with laughter. Mother laughed along with us before she ushered us all toward the middle of the platform as we searched the train windows for a glimpse of Father.

After several minutes, we heard Father calling to us and waving from a window several cars farther down the track. Our little troop fell in behind Mother as we were allowed to board the car and walk down the aisle to where he sat. Perhaps I was just shy since I had been away from him for some time, but I thought he looked even more intimidating than I remembered. In civilian clothes he was a daunting figure, but in his uniform he looked even more impressive. The drab green uniform was stiff-collared with small straps that sat atop each shoulder. His top button was left undone and the large pocketed jacket was belted in the middle. I was fascinated by his short leather boots in which his pants were tucked and, though I was apprehensive, I had to admit that he looked handsome.

Though the visit was short, just a matter of hours, we made the most of every minute as each of us eagerly updated Father on what we had been doing since he had left. He seemed genuinely interested and soaked in every single detail. Inge was now a few months older than the last time he had seen her, and he was visibly surprised at the changes in his youngest child as she sat up, smiled, and cooed at him. Mother made every attempt to make sure the visit was relaxed and upbeat and we were glad to see Father enjoying the pastry we had brought to him.

Since his time was limited, he wasn't permitted to come back to the house. We were fortunate we got to see Father at all, even for such a short time. A month later, my mother received authorization to visit him where he was stationed, and by the spring of 1940, my mother learned she was pregnant with what turned out to be the last of the Röpke children.

But 1940 was a dangerous time to be expecting a child and caring for seven others. During what the British dubbed a "Nickel" raid, Royal Air Force (RAF) planes took off from Feltwell in Norfolk, England in late March, dropping leaflets over Germany hoping to win the war through persuasion of the German citizenry. A Vickers Wellington bomber with her six-member crew was hit by flak, caught fire and crashed in Delmenhorst at 2:00 a.m., a mere 15 miles west of Bremen. It was Easter morning.

A large contingent of military personnel and civilians drove to the crash site the following morning to see the wreckage scattered beside a grove of trees. The front of the plane was unrecognizable, and the fire that had engulfed the fuselage had consumed the bomber's fabric, leaving only its geodesic lattice framework to define its form. The tail gunner's turret was intact, providing curious onlookers a glimpse inside the cramped quarters. The juxtaposition of jagged metal and tranquil foliage was surreal, other-worldly. Photographs were taken of high-ranking Nazis standing in the foreground, politicizing the death and destruction of the prize that was partially pounded into the earth behind them. My mother was shaken. The war had come to our doorstep.

But, while the exultation was memorialized in the Luftwaffe magazine, *Der Adler* —"The Eagle"—Mother winced. This was more than the crash of an enemy aircraft. Lives had been forever altered by the incident. The magazine reported a farmer and his son living near the crash site witnessed the event and held the flyers until authorities arrived. The tailgunner had parachuted safely from the bomber before it crashed, three other crewmen jumped from the burning wreckage sustaining minor injuries. The four men would eventually be taken to different *stalags* as prisoners of war. The two pilots' fates were worse. One lay on the ground, badly injured—he would die a week later from his burns. The other pilot died in the wreckage.

Somewhere in Canada and England, mothers with broken hearts were grieving; in Germany, mothers with beating hearts were taking note, fearing their sons would be next. Young lives lost over nothing more hazardous than attempting to drop pamphlets.

Tons of leaflets were dropped on Germany during the war with questionable results. RAF Air Chief Marshal Sir Arthur "Bomber" Harris, unimpressed by the nickel raids, said, "…the only thing leaflet raids would achieve would be to supply Germany with toilet paper for the rest of the war!" Apparently other military brass concurred. Sustaining more and more losses dropping leaflets, British bombing raids began in Germany, and Bremen was targeted often. Though British air raids were mostly confined to nighttime, Mother was not about to be taken by surprise. Her main focus was keeping all her children safe and she wanted to be sure she knew where we were every moment. While I was at home with Mother each day with Waltraut and Inge, the older children were in school half a day (school was held in the mornings one week, the next week it was rotated to afternoons), but she insisted they come home as soon as school was dismissed for the day. There were to be no side trips.

Just as school was still in session, shops, banks, and life in general were all still open for business. Living in the shadow of war meant we all attempted to live life as normal as possible despite disruptions. We didn't have refrigeration, so the daily trip to the market for perishable foods meant that one of the older children was left in charge of the younger ones at home while Mother and Günter or Karl-Heinz went together to make the purchases with our ration cards. And anytime we left the house as a family, we paired up, held hands, with Mother constantly admonishing us to, "Stay close together."

Like most children, we always enjoyed playing outside. Our neighborhood was lined with numerous two-story detached houses nestled close to another. Each house had a little yard, and we loved rolling around in the grass or playing tag, and with so many siblings, there were always plenty of playmates. The Müllers lived two doors down from us and had two children—*such a small family!* A son and daughter, Manfred and Uta, who were about the same ages as me and Karl-Heinz. We liked inviting them to join our large play group, and our mothers would often find us in the street in front of our houses playing hopscotch. Manfred and Karl-Heinz were always challenging each other to a race, while Uta and I did our best to keep up. I suppose it was fair to say they were our best friends and having them in our neighborhood made the days seem long, sunny, and full of games. But by the Summer of 1940, our mother made it known we could no longer play outside. It was just too dangerous.

Mother was also constantly reminding us to stay quiet, not to say certain things. For years, she and Father had seen the effects of sharing an opinion (especially an unfavorable opinion) of the Nazis or of Hitler. People disappeared as a result. Now that she was the sole parent responsible for what her children heard and might say in public, she became increasingly cautious. She knew the importance of keeping her thoughts to herself to protect her family and she warned us often that we should do the same. We didn't own a radio since anyone caught listening to a foreign broadcast could be jailed or have rations reduced. We would have been totally ignorant of news had it not been for the whispers of neighbors. Mother made sure those whispers rarely reached our ears for fear we would innocently pass that news along. We were, after all, just kids.

It would have been easy for us to shrug those warnings off. We didn't know the unnamed people rumored to be missing or "relocated." But, in the coming months, we would.

Our first introduction to remaining mute was delivered in the form of a letter from our father. All Mother explained to us from his writing was that his "cousin" was coming to stay with us for a few days. I remember Günter's blank expression when Cousin Klaus came knocking on our door by week's end. This was not a relative my oldest brother remembered meeting. Klaus was in his mid-30s, a little disheveled, but had a quiet, pleasant demeanor. He greeted each of us with little elaboration and gladly accepted Mother's offer to bed down in our basement.

Klaus rarely took his meals with the family. He preferred, instead, to eat by candlelight in the basement near his makeshift cot. "I don't want to be a bother," he would tell the boys when they tried to convince him to eat with us. "I have business in Bremerhaven, so I'll have to be leaving soon." But, kids or not, somehow we sensed that wasn't exactly a true story.

In our big bed upstairs, long after we were to have been asleep, Helga and Elfrieda whispered their speculations about our "cousin" and claimed Günter and Karl-Heinz had somehow "discovered the truth."

"He's from Poland," Helga said with hushed authority.

"Why is he in Germany?" Elfrieda turned on her side.

"Escaping."

"To *Bremerhaven*?"

Helga let out an exasperated sigh, "No, silly. That's just the story he's telling. I don't know where he's going. Maybe America."

"Is he a Jew?"

"Günter didn't know," Helga stared at the darkened ceiling of our bedroom. "But, if we are asked, we are just to stay he's our cousin who is visiting… whoever he is."

The next morning, Klaus had come upstairs for breakfast as we were getting ready to go play with Manfred and Uta at their house. Before he had time to make his way back to the basement, the front door was pushed open and Manfred and Uta Müller rushed in. They stopped in their tracks, staring at the stranger in the next room.

Mother cut her eyes to Klaus, picked up Inge and quickly stepped in to greet our friends, "Good morning, children! I'd like you to meet Dirk's cousin, Klaus. He's our houseguest for a few days. Klaus, this is Manfred and Uta."

With bread in one hand and coffee in the other, Klaus merely nodded politely, "Nice to meet you both."

The Müllers nodded quizzically and were rushed out the door with the rest of us the next minute. Looking back, I only caught a glimpse of Mother and Klaus exchanging a glance before the door closed behind us. By the time we came home from the Müller house that day, Klaus had gone. Mother never mentioned him again, but I could tell she was growing more cautious of our friends and neighbors.

The other reminder to be restrained came from my oldest brother. Günter had a friend in school named Josef Kohler. Josef was a feisty boy who was the class clown. He was often the first to raise his hand to answer a question his teacher would ask, the first to volunteer to read a passage from a book, the first to tell a joke to his circle of friends. One day, Günter came home from school with a story that made my mother catch her breath.

"Mutti!" Günter spat out between gulps of air as he threw open the front door. It was obvious he had forced my other siblings to run home so he could share news. "You'll never believe what has happened!"

Mother stepped back from the swinging door and placed her hand over her growing midsection, protective of the child she carried. She shook her head, ushered an exhausted Karl-Heinz and Elfriede in through the wide open entrance, and motioned for Helga to follow into the hallway. They all made their way to the living room and fell onto the sofa, scowling at Günter who was pacing the floor.

"Slow down, Günter. You've worn your brother and sisters out. Would any of you like some milk?"

Everyone else nodded gratefully and followed Mother into the kitchen as Günter lagged behind, incredulous that he wasn't being granted the attention he felt he deserved. "No, no! This is important!" He ran his hands through his hair impatiently, ruffling his normally perfect coiffure.

As we all gathered around the table, Mother began pouring glasses of milk for all of us. I watched with amusement as Günter bobbed behind her as she made her way from one end of the kitchen to the other and back again.

"You remember I told you what Josef Kohler said earlier this week at school?" Günter's hands spread in animation as the words gushed out. "How his mother said the Nazis were going to kill us all if they didn't stop fighting and that his dad should just leave his post with the Army and come home before he got killed, too, and—"

"*Günter! Hush!* Do you want someone to hear you?" Mother came to a complete stop between the two rooms to face her son, almost spilling one of the glasses of milk in her hand.

"But, Mutti!" Günter moaned with exasperation over the interruption. "*I* didn't say it! I'm just telling you what *Josef* said."

Mother didn't look very happy, but gave us our drinks and sat down herself to hear the rest of the story Günter was so anxious to tell.

"*Sooo…* this morning Josef didn't come to school and one of his friends said that *he* heard our teacher tell another teacher that Frau Kohler had a visitor in the middle of the night. Our teacher said it was the Gestapo. I bet it has Heinrich Himmler himself!" Günter finally plopped down in a chair, his brief news bulletin complete.

Just the mere mention of the Gestapo captured the attention of everyone older than me sitting around the table. But, even I knew instinctively from their reactions that this was not good. Mother was visibly upset and she immediately began explaining to all of us again, from the oldest to the youngest, how we couldn't trust anyone since informants were everywhere; that we should never say anything or bad things might happen to our family.

As it turned out, Josef never did come back to school, and we never heard what happened to him and his mother. Mother had been right. There must have been an informant among the teachers or school personnel she had known and trusted for years, and she found that thought very unsettling. From that minute until the end of the war, whenever Mother wanted to remind us the dangers of saying things we shouldn't, Josef Kohler's name was always invoked.

Another new rule Mother put into place concerned how we slept. Since British bombers were flying missions more and more frequently, we never knew when the air raid sirens might sound and we would be sent running for protection. We needed to be ready to go at a moment's notice, so every night we slept fully clothed. We did, at least, get to take our shoes off before going to sleep, but each pair of shoes had to be near the bed so we could find them and slip into them quickly, ready to run.

The cities of Bremen, Bremerhaven and Hamburg are within relatively short distances of one another and each suffered through massive airstrikes. The problem was, we never knew if the planes were meant for our city or the next. So anytime the sirens blared, we didn't gamble our lives by guessing which city was the intended target; we simply ran. It happened often.

I cannot begin to describe how frightening it was to lay down night after night wondering if dawn would find me in bed or fleeing for my life. One night, long after my sisters were breathing deeply and evenly, I quietly lay wide awake, my heart beating loudly at every faint sound heard in the distance. I strained my senses, sure I would be able to detect the sound of approaching planes, only to slowly fall into a deep sleep. Sometime later, the air raid sirens began their warning without interrupting my slumber and I alone was left behind in the house in the midst of the confusion. Then I woke up and realized… it had all been a dream.

But, that very same week in June, my dream became reality and I was determined not to be left behind. We had all finally drifted off to sleep when the slow familiar buildup of the sirens began and woke us. The first siren meant the bombers were coming and we knew we had very little time to seek shelter. Mother shouted at us to put on our shoes. I scurried around in the darkened house, my pulse racing, and my breath coming in short, heavy bursts. I felt sheer terror. We each grabbed someone else's hand in the darkened house and ran as quickly as we could in pairs down the stairs, into the hallway and to the wooden front door, exhausted from yet another night without rest, but driven on by pure adrenaline.

We didn't have far to run. The underground bunker/bomb shelter erected two years before was located in the middle of our neighborhood, encircled by our home and several other brick homes on our street. Within a few minutes we were approaching the bunker. The long, flat structure was built of reinforced concrete with stairs that led from street level to the large "basement" below. As we made our way down the shelter steps, I looked down the avenue and saw other families who lived farther away from our neighborhood rushing headlong toward us. Everyone seemed dazed as they made their way to the building, and soon a bottleneck developed as the very young and the very old or infirm slowed down progress. I gripped Elfriede's hand tighter as I focused once more on reaching the heavy steel door ahead of us at the bottom of the stairs.

The door resembled that of a bank vault. Large and thick, it was edged in rubber so it would be airtight once it was shut and locked. Hitler Youth, Block Leaders, and the Shelter Warden had been the first ones at the bunker to open the door for the onslaught of people, and they encouraged us all to move to the farthest sections of the multi-room bunker so more people could squeeze in.

Eerily lit, the inside of the bunker resembled a huge basement with several rooms that felt cool and insulated with its concrete walls and floor, and concrete benches lined the interior. A hushed reverence seemed to fill the room as everyone huddled together seeking comfort from the impending danger. A few minutes later, after my family sat down in one corner, the second warning blared outside above our heads in the nearly deserted streets, sounding slightly muffled and ghostly. It was a reminder that everyone should now be in the bunkers. I heard adults and children alike near the entrance imploring latecomers who were now sprinting for their lives toward the bunker, "Hurry! Get in!" Some of them made it before the doors had to be closed, some of them did not.

The war became personal as I sat in that bunker. The explosions outside, from ground to air or from the sky to the earth, battered the city, shaking dust from the ceiling over our heads. The lights blinked and I prayed they would remain on. I shook uncontrollably, spooked by the hum of the planes as they approached, grimacing at the sound of the bombs dropping and hitting something off in the distance. I envied one-year-old Inge's ability to sleep through much of the tumult since the rest of us were old enough to recognize that death could touch us at any moment. And we remained in that suspension between life and potential death for hours before we were allowed to venture back up to the street again.

A few hours later, the third and final siren sounded the all clear, but we remained in the bunker until the Shelter Warden opened the door, went up to the street, and gauged whether he deemed it safe for us all to return home. We were in no hurry to leave. There had been times when we had left prematurely only to run back in again moments later as more planes headed our way.

Relieved when the horror was finally over, I dreaded stepping up onto the street, unsure what I would find. Leaving that bunker was another of those memories I will never forget. The first rays of the morning sun were peeking up over the horizon, kissing the surroundings in shadow and light. Rubble dotted our neighborhood; some houses sustained damage, others did not. But what is burned into my mind most of all were the bodies. Individuals who didn't make it into the bunker in time lay crumpled on the street. So near salvation, they made every effort to reach safety before succumbing to death. Some stared lifelessly up at us as we picked our way through the debris and damaged street to our home. Mother warned us to stay clear of the dead, not to touch them. It was surreal and my stomach reeled at the sight. I tried to avert my eyes, but since I had to follow Karl-Heinz and the others and watch where I stepped, seeing the dead, battered bodies was unavoidable.

Previous bombings had left our house relatively unscathed, but not this time. From where we stood on the street, we could see that several windows had glass panes cracked or blown out completely. As we drew nearer, the boys ran around the back of the house and could see some damage to the roof. When we entered the house, we discovered we were also without power and water. Mother took charge and gave everyone a job. The boys were to search inside and out for any materials they could find to board up the windows and patch the roof. What they couldn't find, they were to ask about from our neighbors, and that meant anything that would help with repairs. Mother had the girls start cleaning since the dust from outside and splintered wood from our windows blanketed surfaces upstairs and down. We righted toppled furniture and picked up broken glass. It seemed futile. We might clean and repair, but how long would it be before we were bombed again and had to repeat the entire process?

Months passed. While *we* weren't fully educated on Hitler's reach, the world was painfully aware that the Nazis had invaded Denmark, Norway, France, and much of Western Europe. The Battle of Britain had begun, the Luftwaffe's Blitz was bombarding London and other sites in the UK, and the RAF had instituted bombing missions over Berlin. In mid-November 1940, Coventry, England was almost utterly destroyed by three hundred German bombers. At the same time in Bremen, my mother was seven months pregnant and the British were once again flying over Germany. But this time, they were doing so with a renewed determination, no doubt, in retribution for Coventry. It would be a November we would never forget.

On a cold evening in late November 1940, we were at home when the first air raid siren's sad moan filled the night air. After we hastily donned our coats, Mother grabbed Waltraut's hand while Günter held little Inge's, and the rest of us paired up in quick succession. We threw open the front door and began running across the street toward the bunker. Because Mother was only a few weeks away from giving birth, she and Waltraut were not able to keep the same pace as the rest of us and they were soon lagging behind. Günter and Karl-Heinz turned their heads toward her, yelling and urging her on. We were nearly at the bunker. And then it happened. Mother tripped and fell.

We were surrounded by people, all swiftly making their way to the safety of the shelter. But as if we were a single unit, my brothers, sisters and I stopped immediately and returned to our mother's side amidst the utter confusion. The sirens blared as a few individuals knelt beside Mother to help, while other people gathered around us encouraging us to get into the bunker.

"She needs a doctor," someone yelled out to the crowd. "Is there a doctor?"

None was found, but one woman stopped and made her way through the stream of humanity, "I am a *hebamme!*"

She and a few other selfless individuals attended Mother as she lay sprawled in pain in the middle of the street. Despite our protests, my siblings and I were ushered away by strangers and neighbors toward the bunker. Mother nodded, assured us she would be fine, and sternly told us to get to safety. We were crying, almost hysterical; none of us wanted to leave Mother. She looked so vulnerable. She was pregnant, injured, writhing in pain and she was not only exposed to the elements, but also to the impending wrath of Britain's RAF. Even though we weren't sure what we could do to help, we were sure Mother needed us. We knew we needed her. She was our rock, and her strength and soothing words always helped us get through another night of air raids.

As we neared the entrance to the shelter, I turned in time to see Mother still lying where she had fallen in the street. I asked God to protect her. The midwife and the other people that had stopped to assist her were risking their lives to be caught out in the open, but they remained by her side even as I was taking another step lower into relative safety. Soon, I was too low to see the street and we were quickly directed to one of the rooms to the left of the entrance.

I didn't think the commotion surrounding her fall had lasted long, but we had only been in the bunker for a few minutes when we heard the second siren. I burst out crying knowing by experience what that second siren meant: everyone should be in the bunker, the planes were upon us. A few minutes later, the Shelter Warden was locking the airtight door. Elfriede tried to calm me, but I was inconsolable. I had seen, we had all seen, what happened to those who didn't make it into the bunker in time.

It was another long night spent in the bomb shelter, and my siblings and I were nearly sick. We cried until we were exhausted, and the terrifying sounds of war outside made our fear and worry almost palatable. It helped that Manfred, Ute, and their mother sat beside us and did their best to keep us occupied, but time crawled by. As blasts continued overhead, no amount of consoling could keep my mind off of what might be happening to my mother on the street above. I suppose it might have occurred to Günter or Helga since they were the oldest, but I never once considered what might happen to the baby Mother was expecting in two months. My main fears focused on Mother's injuries and whether she could survive at all on the street outside as bombs rained down on top of us all.

Sometime during the night, the final siren sounded the all clear and the Shelter Warden opened the door and walked outside. While we waited for the Warden's okay to leave, I looked up to see the midwife staring down at all of us. She motioned for us to follow her to another room at the other end of the bunker. Günter and Helga helped us up from the floor and made sure none of our siblings were left behind. We walked the length of the shelter, passing numerous tired faces. As we neared a row of benches, I saw several people huddled on the floor.

"Mutti!" I breathed in the word.

Brought in from the street by her saviors when the Shelter Warden was viewing the damage above, Mother was half-reclining on the floor on a makeshift bed of strangers' coats. She looked up and smiled weakly at us all, then shifted to uncover a small bundle nearby.

The midwife took in the confused looks on our faces and smiled. "You have a new brother!"

FOUR
A CHILDHOOD STOLEN
1941—1942

By the Summer of 1941, Egon was still a small baby, but Mother felt much better about his health. The midwife and another woman came home with us the night of his birth and stayed for a few days. The midwife continued on with us the longest, looking after Mother and Egon, while the other woman saw that the rest of us were fed and kept occupied so Mother could recuperate. The midwife commented that Egon was so little he could fit into a cigar box! Years later, long into his adult years, I look at the strapping man he became, remind him of that comment, and we both laugh.

It was said that Hitler loved children; after all, they were the future. Having abolished all other adolescent programs during the 1930s, a new law in 1939 made it mandatory that pre-teen boys and girls join the Hitler Youth organization. Parents were warned that failure to do so meant their children could be taken from them and placed in government-run orphanages. As a result, the Hitler Youth became the largest youth organization, not just in Germany, but in the world.

The program was touted as a means of insuring children of the Third

Reich were strong and healthy. Boys joined the German Young People at age 10 and then the Hitler Youth at 13. Ten-year-old girls first joined the League of Young Girls and later the League of German Girls. The boys' programs specifically focused on physical fitness activities, but those activities had a decidedly militaristic bent: marching, grenade throwing, and pistol shooting. And while girls had to be active, too, their swimming, marching, and running feats were combined with much more domesticated tasks as well. The Nazis were grooming unsuspecting boys for the military and girls for life as a wife and mother in the fatherland.

While I don't remember much about Günter's time in the Hitler Youth, I do recall a little about Helga's. In the Summer of 1941, she was a new member in the League of Young Girls and one of her main duties was to be an aide in hospitals. She had to wear a striped uniform, which seems appropriate now since her position was comparable to a candy striper in the U.S. Helga was not excited about that job or any other duty the program had in store for her, and I could understand why. For instance, our family didn't own a car, so getting around the city meant we had to walk. But Helga and the rest of her friends in the League of Young Girls had to line up and march wherever they went. They truly had marching orders, and even as a young child I remember thinking how much they reminded me of soldiers. Maybe that's why Helga was always just a little rebellious as she grew up. She had no say in so many areas of life, particularly being in the Hitler Youth, and she desperately needed an outlet to express herself as an individual. Of course, as a kid, I just thought she was mean!

So, while the barrage of British bombing missions over Bremen intensified through that summer and we struggled through debris and fear, it became harder and harder to reconcile the rosy picture painted for the future of German youth, much less the present. Being confined to the indoors because the outdoors was too dangerous was no life for children. But then, living each night in complete terror should not have been typical either. I was living in a stolen childhood.

Watching my mother bear the load of caring for us all each day, I felt guilty when I caused Mother any additional worry or trouble. Unfortunately, for the next few months I didn't seem to be able to avoid causing her extra headaches. As Mother often said about bad news, it seemed my issues all "came in threes" and all three of my problems involved my leg.

The first of my calamities happened that Fall. With the coming of autumn, cool days turned to even cooler nights and when we weren't sitting around the kitchen table, we were dragging our chairs around the potbelly stove in the middle of the kitchen. We kept a fire burning in the stove to heat the house, upstairs and downstairs, and to cook all our meals on its surface. In addition, Mother always kept a kettle of water on the stovetop so we would have hot water ready for meal preparation or for our weekly baths.

On one particularly chilly evening, there were several empty chairs around the stove. There was rarely that much room near our main heat source, so I took full advantage. I sat down in one of the chairs to get warm and used another as a footstool. Stretching out my legs, I crossed my ankles and tilted my head back. It was deliciously warm, and for a moment the war was forgotten. Helga was sitting nearby, idly watching Waltraut and Inge—then three and two years old respectively—toddle around the room. Karl-Heinz sat down beside me, winked, lifted his feet toward the wood-filled stove, and wiggled his toes, soaking in every wave of heat emanating from the fire.

The kettle quietly whistled, its steam lifting toward the kitchen ceiling. It was a quiet, peaceful moment in time and I was so content, my eyelids grew heavy. Elfriede walked in, breaking our repose, and reached over me to take the kettle off the stove. She grabbed the handle, but somehow it slipped from her hand and the kettle teetered sideways on the edge of the stovetop in a momentary balancing act. Gravity finally won, causing the kettle to fall backward toward the floor and, before I could react, boiling water arced through the air and onto my leg.

I didn't realize I had screamed, but I must have done so because Mother appeared by my side as if by magic. Everyone mobilized immediately. Helga

—her hospital experience coming into good use—fell to her knees helping Mother tend to my leg, Günter grabbed the baby and the little girls to keep them out of the way, Karl-Heinz cleaned the water from the floor and Elfriede tried to simultaneously soothe and apologize to me, over and over again.

It was my first trip to a hospital and while I might have enjoyed all the attention under different circumstances, I was in enough pain that I just wanted to sleep until the throbbing was over. And to make matters worse, I had to remain in the hospital by myself for a couple of weeks since it was against hospital rules for family members to stay overnight. Accustomed to a house full of people with whom I was comfortable, it was not easy for me to stay in a ward full of strangers. Mother and one of my brothers or sisters would visit every day and that made the stay more bearable, but I was still anxious to leave. Each morning I asked the nurse if I was going home that day. She just looked at me, brusquely lathered my leg with ointment and applied fresh bandages. I'm not sure she ever answered me. I was beginning to wonder if she even *understood* German.

The only other bright spot during that time was an occasional visit from my uncle, Christian Koelling. My mother's brother had never married, so he had no children and, as result, he doted on me and my brothers and sisters. Uncle Christian was a kind man with a ready smile, very much like his sister, my mother. I remember he loved to make us laugh and he made an extra effort to lighten my mood while I was hospitalized. It was good to see his face and it made me feel a little safer knowing he was living nearby during my father's absence.

Since the pre-war death of their parents, Ludwig and Anna Marie, Uncle Christian continued living in the home in which he and my mother had grown up, and that house was his pride and joy. Family was everything to him and Mother used to say he felt it was his duty to honor their parents by caring for their house as they would have. In peacetime that might have meant routine maintenance, but in the early 1940s that increasingly meant he was patching and repairing and rebuilding. He even helped the boys on our own house after it suffered damage. The boys learned their finer carpentry skills from our father, but they learned to repair a house from Uncle Christian. I was glad he had taken the time to see me. It was a reminder that family stays together, just as Mother so often repeated to us.

As if my first accident-turned-hospital-stay wasn't enough to disrupt our lives more than necessary, it wouldn't be the last time I made the same trip, again, for my leg. I'm not even sure how it happened, but one day I realized I had cut my leg. It seemed insignificant at the time, but I could see that Mother was getting more and more concerned about it as it became more red, swollen, and hot to the touch. No doubt, the ever-present dust and bacteria in the streets had gotten into the cut.

Each day Mother cleaned the wound as well as she could with whatever she had in the house, and each day she looked at it, hopeful the swelling had gone down. When I began running a fever and the swelling get worse, she and Elfriede took me back to the hospital over my objections. I had been there before and wasn't anxious to be away from my family, particularly when the sirens went off and I had no family beside me while the aircraft flew over.

A doctor looked at my leg and told Mother I had some type of Bein Rose and it was communicable. I not only had to be hospitalized so they could monitor my progress and give me medication for the leg infection, I also had to be completely isolated from others until I was no longer contagious. Visitors were prohibited. The droning of planes and the uncertainty of living until morning was dreadful when I was surrounded by family and friends, but it was nothing compared to being totally "alone" in a hospital ward. At the sound of aircraft flying overhead, my shrieks echoed off the walls, I shut my eyes tightly together and buried my sobs in my pillow.

I don't remember how long I stayed in the hospital, but it was considerably longer than when my leg had been burned. My eventual homecoming was joyous and, as I was greeted by all my siblings, I silently promised myself I would never be separated from my family again and I never wanted to see my mother upset or worried about me again.

It was, therefore, almost inconceivable that I could have any other mishaps. After all, I had seen enough of the inside of a hospital and I was now being overly cautious. Being enrolled at school for the first time was a nice diversion and I was excited. Our school was about a twenty-minute walk from our home, but I thought every minute of that walk was fun. I suppose I finally believed I was much more mature since I was leaving my mother and younger siblings behind at home to join my older brothers and sisters to go to school. Just getting out of the house, trying to live a normal life by doing something as simple as attending school was liberating.

Manfred and Uta Müller walked to school with me and Karl-Heinz. We either played games or laughed and talked during the entire journey. Helga and Elfrieda kept a close eye on us as we walked along, even though they were also chatting with their own friends. But Günter was totally oblivious to us since he was occupied with impressing the latest of his female admirers.

Our red-brick school building stood high above the street, paper cutouts of angels and stars taped to each window pane attesting to the painstaking labor of the students within. The entrance to the main hall had two large wooden doors that could only be reached by climbing a long set of steps from the roadway. Every day, eager to be the first to reach the top of those stairs, Karl-Heinz, Manfred, Uta and I challenged each other to a race to the top. Since Uta and I were younger, we never won the challenge, but we enjoyed seeing who would finish third and fourth.

It was inevitable, I guess, knowing my track record during the last few months, that my leg would once again be the recipient of yet another scar. While finishing fourth for the second time that week during the race up the school stairs, I managed to trip on the next-to-the-last step. Almost at the door, Karl-Heinz turned around just in time to see me fall, arms flailing, and land awkwardly on the concrete steps. He and what seemed like the entire student body soon surrounded me, pulling me to a sitting position, brushing the dirt from my clothes and "oohing" and "aahing" over my perpetually-scraped leg. I was mortified. Not only had I just shattered my self-image of a responsible school-aged girl, but it appeared that everyone had witnessed my graceful entrance to school. I also knew I was going to be giving Mother another reason to worry, and *that*—more than my injured leg—made me want to cry. Karl-Heinz and the Müllers were very sympathetic; I'm fairly certain Helga rolled her eyes.

Minutes later, a nurse was greeting me at the hospital. "Edith! How is my *mein liebchen* today?"

I wasn't surprised the hospital staff knew me by sight when I arrived there… again. I merely pointed to my wounded leg and she smiled. "We're going to have to give you your own room if you keep falling down and hurting that leg. Let's take a look at it."

She poked and prodded before putting her hands on her hips and winking at me. "I say three stitches will be the remedy and you should be as good as new." Thankfully, no overnight stay was necessary. Mother was relieved, Karl-Heinz admired my stitches and Helga muttered something under her breath that involved the word, *"Ungeschickt."*

Though I enjoyed school tremendously, as most first-timers do, I was, like all other school children, most happy when school was dismissed for something special. And one such occasion occurred when it was announced we would all be attending a parade. It was very exciting. In addition to schools, all businesses closed for the day and it was mandatory that we go. I stood on the side of the main roadway in Bremen with my family and watched as uniformed soldiers marched by; Nazi flags were flown from the buildings and spectators waved them with exuberance. Hitler Youth participated, walking behind marching bands and cars filled with VIPs.

There was plenty of pageantry, both colorful and joyous. The swastikas with their red and black colors hung everywhere. Soldiers stood watch, large guns slung over their shoulders or ready near their hands. I could hear the excitement of the crowd as a long open car came nearer and soon everyone began extending their arms in a salute. Whether from fear, adulation, or simply the opportunity to see someone famous, the crowd reacted in unison. Adolph Hitler stood in the car, looking extremely tall to someone my age. He was stoic and stiff as he extended his arm in response to the crowd's salute.

It is a memory that has stayed with me to this day, but as vivid as the memory is, I cannot find record of it in any news article, photograph, video or Internet search. Hitler scheduled and then cancelled a visit to Bremen in 1939. I found references to Hitler visiting Bremen in the mid-thirties with a parade held in his honor at that time through the city center. So, had Hitler's visit to Bremen on that occasion been retold so often by others that it has become entangled in my mind with things I saw and experienced as a schoolgirl? Had I merged the parade I witnessed when I was young with the parade he was actually in years before that? I no longer know. But, either way, the image has haunted me into adulthood.

After invading Yugoslavia and Greece earlier in 1941, Hitler set his sights on the Soviet Union and attacked. But in December, whispers around our neighborhood were at a fever pitch. The Japanese had attacked Pearl Harbor and Germany had declared war on the United States. The Allied Forces would have a new country's might joining them, and we could only guess that the British would welcome the extra air power.

As 1942 dawned, we still feared the British bombers after the sun went down, but now the United States Army Air Force (USAAF) began using their air power over German skies during daylight hours. It became more and more difficult to pretend life could continue with any sense of normalcy. School dismissed for the summer and Mother doubted they would open their doors again for the next term. Attending church was too risky and even going to the market each day was a terrifying ordeal. We were more confined than ever, sprinting to the bunker more often and never really getting any rest, by day or night. It was exhausting.

Then on May 30, 1942, Cologne, Germany was bombed by the British in what I learned as an adult was called the "Thousand Bomber Raid." Cologne was the first such raid, but it wouldn't be the last. The city was crippled and a large segment of its population fled afterward. Cologne lay 312 km (194 miles) southwest of Bremen and our city leaders had grave concerns that Bremen might suffer the same fate. Their fears were substantiated by pamphlets dropped over Germany by the RAF that read:

"We are bombing Germany, city by city, and ever more terribly, in order to make it impossible for you to go on with the war. That is our object. We shall pursue it remorselessly. City by city; Lubeck, Rostock, Cologne, Emden, Bremen, Wilhelmshaven, Duisburg, Hamburg—and the list will grow longer and longer. Let the Nazis drag you down to disaster with them if you will. That is for you to decide. We are coming by day and by night. No part of the Reich is safe. People who work in [factories] live close to them. Therefore we hit your houses, and you" [A. C. Grayling, "Among the Death Cities: Is the Targeting of Civilians in War Ever Justified?", page 43.]

Kinderlandverschickung, the relocation of children to the safety of the Germany countryside, had been in place for several years, but my family had not been affected before. But now, with air raids coming both day and night, it had finally become imperative to protect as many children as possible from being killed in air raids, and since our family was large, it made sense to find some place to relocate at least a few of us. Rural areas were not being bombed, so it would be considerably safer if we stayed with families there instead of in Bremen. Though it was an economic burden for foster parents to take in children, those providing temporary homes to displaced children received those children's allotment of ration cards and a government subsidy to defray the cost of caring for them.

My younger siblings were to remain with Mother and Günter in Bremen, but Helga and Elfriede were sent to stay with a family in one direction while Karl-Heinz and I were sent off in another direction. None of us were happy about splitting our family up, but as with so many other aspects of our lives, we had little choice in the matter. It was done in the name of keeping us safe, but doing so meant we would not be together and we would not know how each of us were faring every day. After my trips to the hospital, I had vowed to never leave my family again and, yet, here I was months later, being sent to live with total strangers.

Karl-Heinz and I had been assigned to live in the Black Forest in southwestern Germany, just north of the Swiss border. Mother put on a brave face as she took the two of us to the station where we were to board one of several trains leaving Bremen with hundreds of other children bound to the countryside to meet foster families. None of the parents were allowed to travel with us. They were instructed, instead, to hand us over to a government official who would check us in and supervise us during the trip.

"Now, Edith, I can't go with you, so I want you and your brother to mind your foster parents while you are away from home," Mother told me.

"But, Mutti, I don't want to go! I want to stay with you!" I said through a curtain of tears as I stood on the platform waiting to board our train. "How will we know where to get off and who will meet us when we get there?"

Mother was not comfortable with the situation either, but she tried to paint it in the best possible light. She pointed to an older woman in a tightly-buttoned-up uniform. "Do you see that nice lady over there? She will be taking care of you and Karl-Heinz and all the other children on the train…."

Looking over at the strict woman holding a long list of names and barking orders to her young associates, Mother's explanation wasn't making me feel any better.

"…You just listen to her and she'll tell you when you need to get off the train. The foster parents will be waiting for you at the station; they'll be very excited to meet you both. The Black Forest is a beautiful place. I promise, you will enjoy exploring it and you'll be safe from these terrible air raids. That's the most important thing, Edith."

A whistle blew and we were told to begin boarding when our names were called. Too soon, our names rang out and I tried my best to dry my eyes as Karl-Heinz grabbed my hand, we hopped aboard the train, and found a place to sit. When the train began slowly moving down the track, I kept my gaze on my mother as she stood waving to us. Soon, she was out of sight and my heart sank.

The trip took a full day by train from Bremen and as we neared our destination, the unfamiliar landscape truly became more and more beautiful with its dark, tall forests. Unfortunately, I was in no mood to admit that and I was incredulous that Karl-Heinz was taking our journey so well. He appeared to believe we were on some kind of adventure.

When we finally arrived at the station, Karl-Heinz and I took each other's hands, as Mother had ingrained in us so often, and stepped onto the platform where we picked up our bags. A uniformed man at the station stood transfixed to the clipboard in his hand as he worked through all the children's names before coming to ours. Rapping his pencil on the clipboard, he called out our names brusquely, peered up to see our raised hands and then scratched a line through our names on his list. Scribbling something else on the page, the man barely looked up as he made cursory introductions between us and assigned foster parents standing nearby. That's when I first realized that Karl-Heinz and I would not be living together under the same roof. We had been farmed out to two different families and that made me more anxious than ever.

I was immediately struck by the differences in our two families. Karl-Heinz's foster parents were rotund, jovial and seemed genuinely delighted to have him moving in with them and their son and daughter. My foster parents were thin and somber looking. I gulped. *Didn't they eat as well as Karl-Heinz's family?* My foster father had a receding hairline and what little hair was left on his head was graying at the temples. His wife was as gaunt as he, with a mass of curls that were graying as well. They did have a daughter who looked to be my age and was also named Edith, but while she and her parents seemed friendly enough, I sensed they were far from excited to be taking me home with them. Of course, it didn't help that I cried the entire time we were at the station.

My intuition was correct. Karl-Heinz and I were living in the same village in the Black Forest, but under entirely different circumstances. While we were both relieved to be away from the constant fear of war raining down upon us each day, that's the only area in which our lives were in sync. Karl-Heinz's family was nice and welcomed him with open arms. That entire summer they went swimming, hiking, and exploring. Karl-Heinz was tanned, rested, and well-fed. His foster family was so nice. *My* foster family was rotten!

Across the same village, I was treated like an outsider, an intruder, and I lived with a spoiled girl who never did her chores, but made sure I got the blame despite the fact that I was doing more than my fair share. In her parents' eyes, their little Edith could do no wrong, despite the fact that she threw tantrums and had no respect for either of them. No summer excursions for us; work was the order of every day. Even sitting at home with them at night, there was no laughter, no talking around the table. I was fed, but the other Edith got much larger portions. I didn't have to share a bed, but there was no giggling shared with my temporary "sister." I actually missed Helga pushing me out of our big bed at home and I definitely missed my mother's gaiety.

I cried often, but they wouldn't allow me to visit Karl-Heinz to make me feel better. I was so miserable, I snuck out of their house anyway on more than one occasion to see my brother and his family. The atmosphere in both homes was like daylight and dark. Karl-Heinz and his family never failed to greet me with a smile, take me in, and fatten me up with something delicious. I didn't want to leave, but then my foster parents would show up on the doorstep with a scowl and I would have to follow them back to their sad household and another day with their Edith. Interestingly, they always knew where they could find me.

We didn't have any communication with our real family while we were away, so having contact with each other was important for both me and Karl-Heinz. We were unaware, therefore, what our Mother and siblings were going through just weeks after our arrival in southwestern Germany.

At the end of June, came a stark reminder why children had been relocated: the third Thousand Bomber Raid was launched and, as feared, its target was indeed Bremen. Mother and my siblings survived, but our house had suffered more damage. Had I known, I would have cried more than I was already crying. Instead, I suffered in silence, saw Karl-Heinz when I could, and prayed to see Mother soon.

The Allied forces continued more intensive bombing campaigns throughout central and western Germany, leaving fewer places unaffected. So, what began as an extended stay for us in the Black Forest ended abruptly several months later when the government decided children weren't safe anywhere, so we should at least be allowed to return home to our families. I was elated. Our foster families saw us off at the station. Karl-Heinz's family waved and wished him well; my family nodded and probably sighed in relief. I know *I* did!

Arriving in Bremen, I was struck by how much more damage there was, even in the residential areas, and Mother told us both how extensive the raids had been since our absence. While living in the Black Forest, I had not missed the sheer terror I felt at the sound of the sirens, but it wasn't long before I was experiencing them all over again.

Christmas 1942 came and went with a solemn air and little celebration, and a few months into the New Year, we received a subtle hint of how poorly the war was going for Hitler. Propaganda Minister Josef Goebbels delivered a speech in February 1943 calling for "total war" and more sacrifices from the German population. Weeks later, Mother accepted a letter from the military: Günter was to report for duty. He wasn't quite fourteen years old.

FIVE
THE EYE OF THE STORM
1943

To say my mother was upset when Günter moved outside Bremen to begin military duty is an understatement. Her moods swung between utter dismay to extreme anger. As the oldest child, Günter had taken on the role as the man of the family after Father was drafted into the Army, despite the fact that Günter was barely in his teens. With Father gone, Mother was distressed to have her firstborn son taken, especially since he was still really just a boy. She was, at least, consoled that Günter was not actually considered a soldier, but was, instead, relegated to shuttling messages, helping civilians relocate, and cleaning up debris after air raids. Still, having him out of the house and away from her watchful eye made her tremendously uncomfortable. She had some measure of trust in her own ability to keep her children safe, but she had no confidence that the Nazi government would do the same.

As suspected, school had not re-opened; it was entirely too unsafe, but at least I had gotten my first year—or most of it—checked off my education list. With school out and Bremen a favored target from the air, our lives took on a new normal: Mother and Karl-Heinz scurried as quickly as possible with our ration cards to get food each day, for the most part we remained indoors round-the-clock, and we were acutely aware that we could be huddling in the bunker any hour. We saw very little of anyone outside our family. Manfred and Uta were sequestered with their mother as well, but at least Uncle Christian walked to see us from time to time to help boost our spirits. Truthfully, I think he yearned for the companionship as well.

Weeks after Günter left, there was a daytime raid that damaged or destroyed many of the neighborhoods surrounding our house, including our school and many municipal buildings. We made it to the bunker and felt fortunate to have survived since there were numerous civilian casualties throughout the city. Frau Müller had heard that one of our teachers and her two children were killed in the basement of their home. The news made my stomach hurt; I literally felt physically ill. Seeing bodies of nameless individuals slumped in the street was frightening enough, but hearing that people I knew were dying was beyond terrorizing.

For the third time during the war, our house sustained heavy damage, only this time it was far worse than it had ever been before. A simple patch job by Uncle Christian and Karl-Heinz would only go so far. Mother got word to Father, who was now stationed in Aachen, and within days he was given permission to leave his office to come home. He arrived, surveyed the damage with Uncle Christian, and they both agreed that the house was beyond repair, especially considering the fact that Bremen would most likely suffer through more bombings. He returned to Aachen the same day on a mission to obtain orders allowing our family to relocate. He promised he would send word to us as soon as possible if he was successful.

The following week our orders arrived at the house. Our family had been directed to leave Bremen for reassignment to Saxony in eastern Germany, which had been spared the bombing the majority of the country had sustained. The larger the family, the more likely permission was given to evacuate, so we would be one of the first families leaving our neighborhood. We were to be provided quarters in Krumhermsdorf, just 24 miles southeast of Dresden, not far from the borders of Poland and Czechoslovakia. I remember being sad and excited at the same time. None of us wanted to leave, but we were also more than eager to escape bombs, death, and fear.

A few days before we were scheduled to leave by train, Günter and Uncle Christian came to help us pack all our furniture, belongings and clothing, while Mother carefully packed every linen, photograph, and piece of china. Those items were to be shipped ahead of our arrival in the east, so when the day dawned for our departure, I walked through the empty rooms of my childhood home and cried along with Mother and every member of my family. That is where the large kitchen table sat where we spent every evening sharing meals, there sat the sofa where we lounged and laughed at Mother's stories, the bedroom where I shared a bed with my sisters. The uncertainty of the day did not escape us. Would we ever see our home, city, or friends again?

Before she closed the front door for the last time, Mother made sure she had all the official identification documents we would each need to travel eastward. We would also need those papers to prove our Bremen citizenship, assuming we eventually returned. Walking outside, we met Uncle Christian and Günter who had come to walk us to the station. As we all stood on the street, looking back wistfully at our house, I felt a lump in my throat. As I tried to blink back tears, Uta, Manfred, and their mother stepped out of their house. Uta walked over to me and cried, and as much as I tried not to, I cried as well. She shook my hand, promised to write to me, and we both swore we would see each other again after the war ended and we moved back to Bremen. Manfred and Karl-Heinz spoke about the things they would do when we returned. I don't think they ever uttered the word "goodbye," saying it aloud made it far too real.

It was time to leave. We waved farewell to the Müllers before turning away and walking with Uncle Christian and Günter to the station. Little was said as we made our way through the crowded platform to our train. When we arrived at the station, there was numerous other large families who, like us, were being ordered to evacuate Bremen.

"I don't want to leave without you, Günter," Mother cried softly as she pushed Egon in his stroller toward the train. Helga held four-year-old Inge's hand, while Elfriede helped Waltraut up the lower step of the train car. Karl-Heinz and I brought up the rear.

Günter tried to act unaffected as he fought back his own tears. "You and the children will be safer in the east and I'll be fine here. I have a lot of duties each day so I'll stay busy and I will be very careful; you shouldn't worry about me. I'm sure to be given leave and then I will visit you all."

Mother nodded her head, but was not convinced. She studied his face, anxious to remember every line and feature so she could recall it at will during the undetermined time of separation.

"*Auf wiedersehen.*" Uncle Christian leaned down and quietly said his farewell in his sister's ear. Mother took his hand and squeezed it. As Uncle Christian lifted the stroller and Egon into the train, Mother took Günter's hand in her own and held it as she stared into his eyes. "We will be back."

Mother ushered me and Karl-Heinz up the steps and then made sure we were all in our seats. Once seated, she finally glanced through teary eyes at her brother and her son standing forlornly on the platform as the engine pulled away to the east and an uncertain future. Her downcast expression was mirrored in each one of our faces. As Bremen receded farther and farther behind us, we all did our share of mourning, but in time we each succumbed to the rocking motion of the train car, the rhythmic click of metal on the tracks, and were lulled into the blissful forgetfulness of sleep.

When we reached Dresden, many of the families riding with us on the train disembarked. Dresden, with a population of approximately 350,000, was Germany's main cultural city, known as much for its art and architecture as its china. It was, fittingly, dubbed the "Florence of the North." Now, thousands of refugees were filling the beautiful metropolis to escape the devastation in their own cities.

Since we had been assigned to live in a rural area outside of Dresden, we changed trains there for the short ride to Krumhermsdorf. Once there, we joined another family from the west as we left the train to await our next set of instructions. We stood in line and a soldier asked Mother for each of our documents. He studied them before nodding and giving Mother directions to the house we were to call "home" for the foreseeable future. Hoping our furniture and belongings had preceded us, we gathered the light bags we had packed for the trip, and began following Mother as she pushed Egon in the stroller.

The countryside was serene, and my eyes drank in the sight of unblemished greenery and quaint buildings. The day was nearing its end and a cool breeze ruffled my skirt as we walked along a quiet country road. Krumhermsdorf was a small village, so we didn't have far to walk before Mother and Helga found the address we had been given.

"Children, I think this is the house we will be living in," Mother said. We all stopped in our tracks and looked up the slight incline trimmed with a line of tall, slender evergreens.

"Oooh!" Inge said breathlessly and we all laughed.

An elegant tan-colored manor with a terra cotta roof loomed ahead, three stories high, and I quickly counted more than a dozen windows framed in white facing us. I was in awe. I leaned into Karl-Heinz and whispered, "Are we going to be living in a mansion?"

Karl-Heinz shook his head in disbelief, "No, silly. Maybe this is the wrong address. Are you sure this is correct, Mutti?"

Mother nodded slowly and motioned for us to follow her up the lawn to the front doors, "Yes, but we will just be guests. Some nice family is hosting us for the time being. Now, everyone be on your best behavior."

As if on cue, the double doors in the center of the house opened and a blond-headed boy, who looked to be about Karl-Heinz's age, skipped out onto the graveled driveway that circled the front lawn. Behind him we could make out a large wooden staircase with a red carpet runner. *Red!* And immediately following the boy was a lovely woman, richly attired in a burgundy dress and matching shoes with a long, triple strand of pearls around her neck. She smiled at her son's antics as she reminded him to wait for her. Trailing behind them was the master of the house and the very sight of him abruptly ended our private conversations.

He was not a tall man, and he was a little overweight for his stature, but his starched Nazi uniform, his angry countenance, and the haughty way he held himself gave off an air of self-importance. His boots crunched in the gravel as he walked with determination toward us. He was studying us with skeptical eyes and a lifted chin. He had measured us and, no doubt, found us quite beneath him. I shifted uncomfortably from one foot to another. He stopped, and the silence was deafening as he looked at each of us in turn. Elfriede cleared her throat nervously.

Mother had warned us often to always give the Hitler greeting whenever we met someone in uniform so, following Mother's lead, we all held out our arms at a high angle and saluted the man before us.

"Heil, Hitler! I am Colonel Pfiffer." the man spoke with gruff authority. "This is my wife, Frau Pfiffer and our son, Michael. You are the Röpkes."

"Yes, sir," Mother said with forced confidence.

He held his hands behind him as he paced back and forth in front of our family. We listened intently to every word as he motioned toward the large dwelling. "This is *Schloss Krumhermsdorf.* My family resides in the manor's first two stories and above our quarters is an attic, which should be a suitable apartment for your family. That's where you will be staying while you are here. You should always enter from the stairs in the back of the house rather than through the front doors. In that way, you will not interrupt our lives and we will not interrupt yours. Your furniture and personal belongings have already arrived and have been taken upstairs for you. There is a small kitchen with a cookstove in your apartment so you will be able to prepare food and will have heat and hot water. Ours is a small village so you will be meeting the *Bürgermeister.* He will be checking in with each of the refugees assigned to Krumhermsdorf. There are trains to Neustadt and to Dresden and a market just down the street. Now, do you have any questions?"

Mother was startled. Helga stifled a giggle. Mother quickly and covertly silenced her with a look before turning her attention back to our host and finding her voice, "Thank you, Colonel Pfiffer. We are very grateful to you for providing—"

"Very well," he interrupted before turning on his heel and practically marching back into the house.

"Please excuse my husband." His wife smiled patiently as her husband disappeared into the manor. "He is a busy man these days," she explained breezily. "If you need any help rearranging any of your furniture or run out of coal for the stove, please let one of our servants know and they'll be happy to assist."

"Danke," Mother thanked her and smiled back.

"And perhaps your boy can come downstairs to play with Michael from time to time." Frau Pfiffer nodded in the direction of her son who had already introduced himself to Karl-Heinz. Though the adults might not be comfortable with the arrangement at hand, the two boys already seemed to be striking up a fast friendship. "He has so few friends to play with here. I know he will enjoy having a little playmate."

"I'm sure Karl-Heinz would be delighted," Mother replied.

"Good. Well, we'll let you get settled in then." Frau Pfiffer snapped her manicured-nailed fingers in Michael's direction and walked back through the double doors in the front of the house.

Michael waved to Karl-Heinz, and Mother motioned for us to follow her to the back of the house to find our entrance to our apartment. We entered a door behind the house and climbed a modest staircase inside the rear of the residence that led up two flights to a roomy attic. When we opened the door to our apartment, we were all delighted. The younger children ran around the rooms, excited to be free to wander, while the rest of us explored at a considerably slower pace.

A small well-equipped kitchen sat at one end of the attic with our table and chairs placed near a coal stove. The middle section of the attic would be our living room even though our familiar sofa, chairs, and *schrank* cabinet didn't quite fill the area. Walking through the living room, we entered another large open room which would serve as our bedroom, but that's when we discovered one little issue.

"Mutti, our big bed is here, but where is your bed and where is the boys' bed?" I said as my shoes clicked on the wood floors and echoed in the almost-empty room.

Mother scanned the rooms again, pondering the problem, taking inventory of the furniture that had been shipped from our home in Bremen. There was one other door off the bedroom, but when she opened that door she found a small bathroom with a sink and toilet. There were no other beds in the attic. "Well, it appears some of our belongings didn't complete the journey to Krumhermsdorf."

"But, where will we all sleep?" Karl-Heinz asked with growing alarm as he glanced at the hardwood planks on the floor.

"Well, all the girls will sleep in the bed as usual, of course. And, Karl-Heinz, you and Egon will just have to sleep across the foot of the bed," Mother decided.

I'm not sure who groaned more: Karl-Heinz or all the girls.

"But, what about you, Mutti?" Elfriede asked.

"I'll sleep in the living room on the sofa," Mother said matter-of-factly.

I doubted the sofa would be very comfortable to sleep on each night, but from its vantage point in the living room, the sofa faced a door and a bank of windows with a view to the west. Helga had already thrown the door open and stepped out onto a balcony beyond to take in that view, and it was beautiful. I followed her outside and relished the cool burst of wind I felt against my face. Despite the housekeeping we needed to do inside, all eight of us were soon standing on that balcony soaking in the peace and quiet. The panoramic landscape was idyllic. The sleepy village and its rolling hills filled the foreground; in the distance, the skyline of Dresden sat just on the horizon. As daylight faded, the lights of the ancient Saxon city twinkled lazily.

I sighed. As fearful as I was of the uncertainty of our future, I was awed by the contrast between my hometown and my new residence. In Bremen, nighttime meant terror and explosions, in Krumhermsdorf, the night was filled with the sound of cattle lowing and the laughter of children playing outside. We had not forgotten we were encircled by war, yet for the time being we were living in a rural paradise. It was like being in the eye of the storm.

In the coming months, we settled into an almost carefree existence. Mother would receive an occasional letter from Frau Müller or Uncle Christian that satisfied her curiosity on life back in Bremen. Not long after we arrived, Günter received leave and was allowed to visit for a few days which buoyed Mother's spirits. I was enrolled in school with my older siblings and when we came home for the day, we could play outside with few restrictions. Had I not seen military personnel and vehicles from time to time, I might have been able to convince myself there was no war being waged in the world. But there were reminders everywhere: homes flew the familiar swastika flags, the village gossip was tempered with fear of the Soviet Red Army and, of course, the stern Colonel Pfiffer lived below us in the manor. I was never sure he liked us, but then I'm not sure he was the type of man to like anyone outside his family. He always exuded an air of superiority and the respect (or fear) that he received from the villagers led Mother to caution us to always be courteous, but to stay clear of him.

Thankfully, Colonel Pfiffer was away from home a lot for what must have been a very active period during his service. Each time he was gone, everyone in the household seemed to breathe a little easier and it was during those absences that Karl-Heinz was most often asked to come downstairs to play with Michael. After he returned from a visit, we would pelt him with questions about the mysterious manor we lived above.

"What does the manor look like, Karl-Heinz?" Elfriede sat him down across from her at the kitchen table one afternoon.

Karl-Heinz grabbed an apple and bit into it, pondering for a good while on how to describe what he had seen. When he finally he spoke, he was concise.

"It's nice."

Helga threw her hands up in exasperation, "We *know* it's nice! Tell us about the rooms and the foyer and the stairs. We want details."

"Well…" He chewed some more and squinted his eyes, staring up at the ceiling, trying to find words. "You saw the red carpet on the stairs from the front doors. There's lots of fancy furniture in every room. I didn't want to sit down anywhere; I was afraid I would get it dirty."

"Mutti!" Helga turned to Mother, imploring her to convince Karl-Heinz to share more information.

"You might as well tell them as much as you know, son." Mother laughed at Karl-Heinz as she shooed Inge and Egon out of the kitchen. "The girls aren't going to leave you alone until they've heard it all."

Karl-Heinz grinned, knowing full well he was torturing his older sisters and loving every minute of the power he held over them. "There are lots of rooms. They have a library with loads of books and the sitting room has one of those big crystal chandeliers and so does the dining room. There was a really long table with china and glasses and more than a dozen chairs, and I saw a big ballroom. There were all kinds of servants working while Frau Pfiffer sat in the library and read and Michael and I played in his room. Oh, yeah, and every wall has great big tall paintings in gold frames. They all looked pretty old to me."

"I wish I could see it." Helga sighed. "I bet it's gorgeous."

Mother looked disapprovingly at her oldest daughter, "You watch what you do here. We are guests and we have been told we are to stay in our quarters. Besides, I have another idea you may like even better."

That announcement got everyone's attention. "I would like to visit Dresden tomorrow. We can attend church and then see the city. I think you'll find, Helga, that Dresden will have more than enough opulence to keep you from running into trouble downstairs."

Helga squealed in delight.

The next morning, we all dressed in our best church attire and boarded the train to Dresden. Most of my recent trips by train had been extremely emotional journeys, so it was nice to have a trip I actually looked forward to. As soon as we stepped off the train in Dresden, I couldn't take it all in. I was accustomed to Bremen's streets being littered with ruins, and its buildings and houses reeling in a constant state of disrepair from the war. Dresden was a city refreshingly free of damage, untouched by the war raging around us.

Mother pointed in the distance to the exquisite Lutheran church where we were going to attend services shortly, and we eagerly marveled at the *Frauenkirche*'s massive dome punctuating the city skyline. We followed the curve of the River Elbe to the city center where the Frauenkirche finally stood proudly in front of us, rising from the stone pavement of the Neumarkt behind the statue of Martin Luther. Walking around the building, my eyes absorbed the sight of the centuries-old baroque architecture and spires as Mother explained its history. I was so excited to be attending services in such a beautiful place that I practically ran in the building before Mother caught me. The eight of us streamed in through the massive doors along with a crowd of other churchgoers and were transfixed by the towering interior facing the altar. It was gold, white, and so richly ornate that I had trouble watching my steps because my head was tilted backward to look up at the walls and ceiling. The choir was accompanied by a massive pipe organ and the music swelled, echoing off the sanctuary's marbled walls. To be truthful, I don't remember much about the service itself, I was so consumed gazing at the balconies and the paintings overhead in the cupola.

Thankfully, we had brought Egon's stroller since we did a lot of walking that day near the river: by the lovely rococo Zwinger Palace and its lavish fountains and gardens, the *Katholische Hofkirche* church with the Dresden Royal Palace on its left and the grand opera building, the *Semperoper*, to its right. It was a beautiful day, the sun smiled down on us and all concerns were forgotten for a time. By evening, we were riding back to Krumhermsdorf, tired, but content. Though we hadn't gone in any of the other buildings besides the *Frauenkirche* that day, I knew Mother would have loved to have toured the *Semperoper* since opera was her favorite genre of music.

Months later, with several of us working odd jobs around the village, we had saved just enough money—combined with some of Father's military pay—to send Mother and two of us to the opera in Dresden. Mother balked at first, but we all insisted she treat herself. Helga even offered to stay with the younger children allowing her to feel free to go. Seeing her protests would not get her very far, she finally chose me and Elfriede to go with her. While I wasn't excited about going to the opera where I would be required to sit quiet and still for who knows how long, I *was* happy to have a reason to dress up, and I was delighted that we were finally doing something that would please my dear Mother and give her something to look forward to besides work and worry.

By the time we arrived in Dresden and made our way to the banks of the River Elbe, the *Semperoper*'s Baroque exterior was bathed in lights, as were the two statues on either side of the main entrance. Mother explained the statues were of famous German writers: Johann Wolfgang von Goethe and Friedrich Schiller, and she pointed out statues of Shakespeare, Sophocles, and Euripides in the niches at the sides of the building. All the while, the statue of Saxon King John stood guard in the front of the Opera house. But as awe-inspiring as the exterior was, the interior was just as magnificent.

Once the doors were opened, Mother, Elfriede and I walked hand in hand up a wide red-carpeted staircase flanked by several pairs of marble columns and wood paneled walls. Large brass chandeliers with white globes hung down from the painted buttress ceiling high above us. I couldn't help but stare. We showed our tickets to one of the hosts and were ushered to our seats on the main floor near the back of the opera house.

"Mutti, how big is this place?" I asked wide-eyed as I turned in my red upholstered seat to take in the massive curved hall that seemed bathed in gold.

Mother laughed. "I'm not sure, but I think there's plenty of room for our big family and several more, don't you?"

I nodded and continued to observe the balconies surrounding us, rising in circular layers to the ceiling. A massive crystal chandelier was centered overhead, framed in painted frescoes, and, directly in front of us, the stage was framed with regal, red velvet curtains with an enormous scalloped valance. As elegant as the interior was, many of the patrons filing in to their seats complemented their surroundings perfectly. While we were wearing our best Sunday clothes, there were some women walking past us who were dripping in jewels set against rich silk or satin dresses as they were draped on the arms of uniformed officers.

As the orchestra began playing, Mother smiled broadly at me and Elfriede, but as the evening wore on, I fidgeted in my seat, squirming out of boredom, eager to be back in the attic at the manor. Time seemed to drag on at an excruciatingly slow pace and I was reminded why I didn't like operas: the music sounded pretty, but I didn't understand a single word they sang!

But as for my mother, she was thrilled to be sharing her passion for opera with two of her daughters. From time to time during the program, I watched her, and there was no doubt she felt she was in heaven as she absorbed her special evening. Her eyes closed at the crescendos and a sweet smile crossed her lips. She was no longer a woman without a home, carrying the burden of keeping her children away from war. Tonight she was transported and no one else existed but Mother and the romantic chords of Robert Schumann.

SIX

ACTIONS AND CONSEQUENCES

1943

With a small, close-knit native population, it wasn't difficult to know who the newcomers were to Krumhermsdorf. After all, the larger cities hosted greater numbers of fleeing families while only our family and a few others from western Germany had been relocated to this rural section of Saxony. So it was easy for the *Bürgermeister* to make the rounds and meet the mothers who were the heads of the non-resident households now calling the town home.

I don't remember his name and I was never really sure if he was actually a locally elected politician or had just been unofficially dubbed the village "mayor," but, either way, the *Bürgermeister* was a likable gentleman who exuded charisma—like all good politicians usually do. He first called on Mother a month or so after we had moved in and, afterward, she would run into him from time to time at school or at the market just down the road. He was a tall, dark-skinned man who appeared to be in his 50s with a perpetual smile, a deep bass voice and a penchant for talking.

He thrived on visiting his "constituents" and enjoyed his position, feeling it his duty to advise, update, or more often gossip with those he met during his rounds. Having new "residents," in the form of evacuees, provided a new audience for his stories, and buoyed his feeling of importance. Mother would always scold Helga whenever she began poking fun at him after he was out of earshot. After all, she explained to her oldest daughter, between the rural locale and the fact that we had no radio, we were starved for any information on the outside world. The *Bürgermeister* was a wealth of information and was becoming a genuine friend.

In sharp contrast to the very personable mayor, our host downstairs was a rude, intimidating man. While his wife was standoffish, she was at least pleasant. Colonel Pfiffer, on the other hand, was simply downright hostile to us all. He never had a kind word to say and he treated us like second-class citizens. Karl-Heinz shared a story or two of playing with Michael in the lavish floors below and being warned by the Colonel in a menacing tone to "keep your voices down" or "running is not allowed indoors." Thankfully, the man's war duties kept him away from home more and more often, leaving the manor with a much more relaxed air when he was not in residence.

I always did my best to stay out of the man's way whenever I was walking on the manor grounds, but when I did venture a peek at him, I never saw him smile. And with the exception of returning Hitler's greeting, the man rarely acknowledged my Mother, much less the rest of us. None of us cared for the man, but Helga, in particular, was most vocal about her disdain for him. She didn't like him, she didn't like his attitude, and she didn't like his rules. I suppose, then, that it was just a matter of time before those two immovable forces—Colonel Pfiffer and Helga—collided.

As small as Krumhermsdorf was, there was still an active Hitler Youth presence even there, and, just as had been the case in Bremen, Helga was required to attend meetings of the League of Young Girls. While there weren't as many girls to befriend in the unit, Helga enjoyed the diversion and was glad to have opportunities to get out of the apartment. One night after attending a meeting in town, Helga made her way back to the manor, running across the manicured front lawn. She should have made her way to the back door and up the servants' stairs to our apartment as usual, but on this particular night she decided against that. "It's dark behind the house, I'm tired and a shortcut sounds good. And, besides... no one will know; the Colonel hasn't been home for over two weeks," she reasoned. Her long-standing desire to see the carpeted staircase and luxurious interiors in the manor, no doubt, played a big role in her decision as well.

So, with lots of bravado and a little bit of spite deep in her soul, Helga gingerly stepped to the front entrance, carefully opened the double front doors, peered around the foyer to make sure no one was nearby and quietly closed the doors behind her. Taking a quick glance around her at the crystal, brocade, and silks she had been dreaming of seeing, she made a mad dash on the tiled floor to the wide staircase bathed in red, taking the padded steps two at a time to the landing... and came face-to-face with Colonel Pfiffer!

We were all sitting around the kitchen table talking when the attic door flew open, Helga entered the room, flushed and wide-eyed, and just as hastily closed the door behind her. Always so confident and a little rebellious, it was odd to see my oldest sister looking shaken and nervous, leaning against the closed door.

"Helga?" Mother asked, taking in her daughter's unusual behavior. "Is something wrong?"

Helga seemed frozen, unable to move away from the support of the hard, wooden door behind her. "I... I came through the manor and up the big staircase."

"Helga! You know we are not supposed to do that; I've warned you repeatedly." Mother stood and placed her fists on her hips. "What if someone had seen you?"

"Someone did." Helga's voice cracked.

That got everyone's attention. Even three-year-old Egon sat perfectly still, innately sensing the tension in the room.

"*Who?*" Karl-Heinz breathed with interest.

Looking a little nauseated now, it was obvious Helga was scared. "I met Colonel Pfiffer on the stairs."

We all reacted simultaneously. Mother was not happy. "What?" she asked increduously; Karl-Heinz was amused, "Wow!"; and Inge made the same comment she had when she first saw the manor, "Ooooh!"

Hushing everyone, Mother led Helga from the door and made her sit on one of the empty chairs around the table.

"Oh, Mutti! That's not all!" Helga struggled to hold back tears and was close to being speechless. I was actually impressed; I didn't know Helga *could* be at a loss for words.

Mother found a cloth and wet it in the kitchen, returning to wipe Helga's face and neck in an attempt to calm her down.

"I was... I was so surprised and scared when I saw Colonel Pfiffer that I... I didn't salute." Helga's voice dropped to a whisper.

I noticed Mother's angry expression suddenly turned to one of worry. "Did he say anything to you?"

Helga shook her head quickly from side to side, "No... *well*... I don't know. He looked so angry... finding me in the house and then when I didn't salute... I just ran up the stairs as quickly as I could to get here."

Mother attempted to reassure Helga that all would be well, but it was obvious she was now as concerned as Helga was scared. She was, however, confident that tonight's incident would keep Helga out of mischief for some time.

Early the next morning as we were finishing breakfast, an unexpected knock sounded on the attic door. Mother actually jumped, but before she had a chance to walk across the kitchen floor to greet our visitor, a dreaded voice boomed from the landing.

"Frau Röpke, I would have a word with you."

"Children, why don't you go to your bedroom and shut the door?" Mother asked calmly as she quickly tidied the dirty plates and utensils.

Helga grabbed Egon's hand, while Elfriede clutched Inge's and they motioned for the rest of us to follow them across the attic to our bedroom. I walked quickly behind Karl-Heinz, my heart beating loudly as if I had been the offender from the night before. Once inside the bedroom, we shut the door and sat quietly staring at one another. Helga was wringing her hands, fearful of the upcoming conversation the two adults would be sharing.

Satisfied we were all stowed away in our bedroom, we heard Mother open the door to the attic and we held our breath, anxiously straining to hear every syllable the two had to say to one another.

"Heil Hitler," Mother greeted him.

"Heil Hitler."

Heavy footsteps echoed on the hardwood floor as the Colonel took a few steps into the kitchen. There were no preliminary pleasantries; as usual, he was all business. "I met your oldest daughter on the staircase downstairs last night. She was told not use that entrance, I believe."

Mother's voice sounded meek after hearing his blustery proclamation, "Yes, Colonel, I have reminded her of that and I am assured it will not happen again. I—"

"And," he broke in, as if he had not heard her response, "your daughter did not salute me."

I heard Mother's intake of breath as she was about to offer some type of defense, but he interrupted her again. His voice rose as he slowly enunciated each word, "Does your daughter not respect this uniform?"

Again, he did not allow Mother time to respond. Instead, his measured footsteps thumped the floor as he paced briefly. He suddenly stopped and *this* time his words were low and menacing.

"If you ever want to see your daughter again, you tell her she had better salute when she sees an officer in the Third Reich."

"Yes, Colonel Pfiffer." Mother's voice quavered slightly as his booted steps caused the floor to creak near the door.

As we sat mutely, listening to the fading sounds echoing on the landing and then the back stairs, Helga buried her face in her hands and quietly wept. She never again darkened the main door of the manor.

I'm not sure whether Colonel Pfiffer was mean by nature or had let power and rank make him so, but I suppose it was fair to say that everyone in Germany was on edge by mid-1943. From the tidbits Mother heard from the *Burgermeister*, the war was not going well and we could tell in our own daily lives that food and supplies were getting harder to come by. Letters from Bremen came less frequently as well. Mother longed for word of home and poured over each letter she received, sometimes reading each letter numerous times to herself before sharing the contents with us. Frau Müller continued to write and remind us all how fortunate we were that we were no longer having to scurry to bunkers at all hours of the day and night, while Uncle Christian's notes contained words of encouragement, a little humor, and less talk of the struggles he must have been enduring alone in his parents' house. Mother always smiled at her brother's writings.

"He desperately misses you all," she would say, holding his letter close to her heart. "But I know Christian, and there's a lot he is not telling me."

Military leaves for Father and Günter were non-existent at this stage of the war and correspondence from them was becoming more and more sporadic as well. Though the government wouldn't admit it officially, civilian travel was discouraged, so going across the country to Bremen to see Günter was not an option. But Father was now living in barracks on the outskirts of Berlin which was situated just 187 km (116 miles) north of Dresden. Having not seen her husband in months, Mother decided to make a quick trip to Berlin in the summer of 1943. Despite the risks, Mother was determined to go before travel was disrupted or totally prohibited, and she knew it would be safer if she only took one of us with her. Helga, who was practically an angel after her run-in with Colonel Pfiffer, volunteered to stay with the rest of us while Mother and Elfriede made the trip by train to Berlin to surprise Father.

Mother suggested that each of us write a short letter which she would take as a gift to Father. Since we were not allowed to go, writing him a letter at least made us feel like we were somehow participating in the journey in some small way, and our thoughts and well-wishes would help convey that. Having the family separated was difficult, but at least we had each other while Father had only a few pictures of us to pin near his bed. I was so excited to be sharing a little about school and life in the village with Father, and I hoped that my letter would remind him of me often. Glancing over at four-year-old Inge's scribbling, I wasn't sure what Father could make of her "message." And as for little Egon's note, it had nothing more on it than meandering lines. I sighed and continued proudly pouring out my heart, writing what I was sure would be Father's favorite note to read.

The day of the trip arrived and Mother's laughter was as contagious as ever. With the exception of our trip to the opera in Dresden, I had not seen Mother so giddy. She had taken our letters, stacked one atop the other, combined them with a few handpicked flowers, and tied them together with a string to make a very handsome presentation for Father. Karl-Heinz carried the two small bags they were taking with them to Berlin and we all chatted happily as we made our way through town to the station. The only thing that dampened our spirits was Elfriede's pointed reminder that she was going to Berlin, which in the relatively short walk to the station was mentioned over and over again until Helga was ready to explode. Though she had been a sweeter, more patient person of late, the "old" Helga made a brief reappearance when she finally listened to as much of Elfriede's bragging as she could stand and blurted out through gritted teeth, *"Enough, Elfriede!"*

Mother was in too good a mood to chastise Helga, and Elfriede was in too good a mood to be bothered, so the outburst faded away as the train whistle shrilled into the sky announcing its departure. Within minutes, Helga was too busy to be aggravated by her younger sister any longer when Egon began wailing at the sudden realization that his mother was leaving him behind. As the train's wheels slowly rotated on the steel tracks, Helga did her best to soothe Egon, but now Inge was joining in the chorus and Waltraut was choking back tears as well. Karl-Heinz actually laughed as Helga and I began running around, herding the little ones toward town and coaxing them into a happier mood. Mother was only going to be gone for two or three days, but I had a feeling it was going to feel much longer for those of us left in the attic.

Father's barracks were located just outside Berlin, so Mother and Elfriede disembarked a few stops before the city itself. Elfriede had been so disappointed about that aspect of the trip when Mother first asked her to go that Mother told Elfriede they might try to find time to visit Berlin for a few hours one day while they were nearby. That appeased Elfriede and gave her something to look forward to in addition to seeing our father. But, though they were a few miles from Berlin, Mother immediately sensed that traveling into the city might not be a good idea.

Already, troops, armored vehicles and military equipment were speeding past them in a flurry of activity. The hum of commotion could only be greater in the German capital. Mother grew more skeptical of visiting the city center. Besides, living in Krumhermsdorf had made us more appreciative of living without air raids and bunkers. If Bremen had been a prize to be bombed, how much more would Berlin be? At the start of the war, the Allies didn't have bombers able to fly long-range trips into Germany to target Berlin, but the *Bürgermeister* had warned Mother that word was they now did. In January '43 and again in April—on Hitler's birthday—the Allies had bombed Berlin and Mother knew all too well the risks involved in being in a city targeted for bombing. She didn't mention her change of heart to Elfriede, but she felt it safer to visit Father and return to Saxony as soon as possible. There would be no visit to Berlin itself.

The two checked into a small hotel several blocks from the Army barracks and, after unpacking their bags, they left on foot, anxious to surprise Father. Armed with the bundle of letters from her children in one hand and her pocketbook and ever-present identification in the other hand, Mother guided Elfriede down the street in the direction of the barracks. Upon approaching the main gate, they stood in line behind other family members who had also come for the weekend to visit a family member.

When they finally reached the gate, a young soldier on duty requested their identification papers and asked who they were there to see.

"My daughter and I are here to see Diedrech Röpke," Mother answered.

Papers were shuffled, the name checked and re-checked and, after several minutes, an unsmiling young man finally answered, "He's not here."

"Oh." Mother was taken aback.

"He signed out this morning." The young man pointed to his records.

"Do you know when he'll be back?"

"He doesn't have to be back for 24 hours."

"Well, do you know where I can find him?"

"Actually, yes." The young soldier answered, scanning his records again. "He's on a visit at an apartment building in town."

"Berlin?"

"No, ma'am, just about two miles down this road." The soldier pointed in the direction from which they had walked.

Mother was relieved. She and Elfriede had traveled a long way only to find him gone, but at least he was still nearby. "Would I be able to have the address? I'm his wife."

The soldier nodded and scribbled the address on a sheet of paper. "You can give your husband's name to the apartment manager and he should be able to tell you which apartment he is visiting."

"Danke," Mother said as she and Elfriede turned around to make the walk back into the residential area.

"Who do you think he is visiting, Mutti?" Elfriede asked as they turned to retrace their steps.

"I'm sure he has several friends he has met while he has been here, and I remember he mentioned an elderly couple in recent letters," Mother told her. "Orphaned as early in life as your father was, I believe he almost thinks of them as the parents he never really knew. I'm anxious to meet them."

Checking the address the soldier gave her, Mother reassured Elfriede they could find the apartment building easily. After a few minutes, they had walked past their hotel and could see several rows of well-built brick buildings several blocks ahead. Though it was within sight, it was getting later in the day and the afternoon sun had heated the air considerably. By the time they found the correct address, they were tired, sweaty, and ready to get in from the sunny street. Entering the lobby of the apartment building, they saw an elderly gentleman sitting behind a counter, his head down as he busily sorted mail.

"Excuse me," Mother said as she approached the counter. "I was given this address at the Army barracks and was told that I would be able to find Diedrech Röpke visiting here."

The elderly man looked up from the letters in his hands and casually glanced up at Mother. "And who might be asking for him?"

"This is my daughter, Elfriede, and my name is Marta. Marta Röpke," Mother answered with a smile. "Diedrech is my husband."

The gentleman didn't answer, but slowly leaned back in his chair, staring quizzically at the woman in front of him. He looked down and placed the letters on the counter.

Sensing he was reluctant to provide the information, Mother asked politely, "Would you mind telling me the apartment number?"

"No," the man said slowly. He peered back up at her.

Twelve-year-old Elfriede cut her eyes over at Mother, mirroring her look of confusion, and shrugged.

"Second floor. 202," he finally conceded.

As they left the lobby and headed for the stairs, Elfriede looked back. The old man was still sitting where he had been, watching them walk away. "He was an odd little man."

Mother giggled. "I suppose the heat is getting to us all." Undeterred and too tired to ponder over the man's behavior, Mother and Elfriede trudged up the carpeted staircase to the floor above.

"202. It must be down here." She beckoned Elfriede to follow her to one end of the slender hallway. They found the apartment number and Mother quietly rapped her knuckles against the door.

When there was no answer, Mother knocked again. *This* time she was sure she heard movement inside and, after another moment, she distinctly heard footsteps approach the door. She knocked a third time.

"Yes? Who is there?" A female voice inquired from the other side of the door.

"My name is Marta Röpke," Mother replied. "I was told I could find my husband Diedrech here."

Without hesitation, the door swung wide to reveal the woman behind the voice. She was not the elderly woman Mother had expected, but appeared to be in her thirties. Clad in a robe, with a mass of tousled red curls surrounding her long, slender face, she held the door open with one hand and swung her other arm wide to welcome her guests into the living room.

"Please, Marta, come in."

They stepped inside the neatly-appointed apartment and glanced around. A comfortable floral-covered sofa and armchair sat in front of an open window with lace curtains fluttering in the warm summer breeze. They walked farther into the room, unsure if they should sit down, waiting for the woman to invite them to do so. Without warning, they heard a door fling open behind them.

They turned to catch a glimpse of a figure racing out of a side room, past the woman and through the open front door in a blur. The young woman had not moved from the doorway, but had now crossed her arms in front of her, her head bowed as she quietly chuckled. For a moment, Mother hesitated. Then, sensing she should follow, Mother ran to the door and peered down the hall to see a man running toward the stairwell. As he turned to sprint down the flight of stairs, she caught a brief look at his profile. She recognized Diedrech immediately. He had been holding a bundle of clothes and a pair of boots close to his chest, and he had nothing on but his long johns.

SEVEN
FIRE AND ASHES
1944—1945

Mother and Elfriede didn't take chase, but instead took their time walking down the hall to the staircase where they made their way to the ground floor of the apartment building. By the time they reached the lobby, Father had, no doubt, thought twice about running into the street in his current state of undress, and had managed to put on his pants and boots. As Mother reached the counter, the old gentleman who had been sorting mail peered up at her with a pained expression and she winced, now seeing his earlier demeanor with newfound clarity. Turning, she faced Father. He was buttoning his shirt with a defeated look on his face and had trouble meeting her eyes, much less his daughter's.

With few words spoken between them, he followed his wife and daughter to their hotel. Elfriede was upset by the events of the last hour, but was almost too stunned to know how to react. Mother was so angry she couldn't speak and Father was so contrite he lagged behind them both in an embarrassed stupor. When they reached the hotel, Mother sent Elfriede on up to their room while she and Father remained in the lobby, tucked away in a corner near the front door away from prying eyes and ears, for a private conversation. Once Elfriede was out of earshot, my level-headed, even-tempered, laughter-filled Mother let my Father have it.

"I'm taking care of your kids and you are messing around here?" She seethed as quietly as possible in the seat next to him.

He didn't respond. What could he say? The evidence was more than circumstantial. He sat with slumped shoulders, his head lowered in defeat.

"Yes, Dirk? Did you say something I missed?"

"Marta, I… I have no excuse."

"No," she answered, her spine straight, her eyes bright with indignation. She couldn't look at him, but stared through the plate glass window at the front of the hotel lobby toward the hustle and bustle of the street beyond. "No, you do *not* have an excuse. There *is* no excuse. You have betrayed me and you have betrayed your children."

Awkward minutes passed with neither of them speaking.

Mother broke the silence first. "Does she know you have a wife?"

He nodded.

"Does she know you have a *family?*"

His voice was so hushed it was almost inaudible, "Yes. Well, I… I told her… um…." He stumbled over his words.

"Yes?" she prodded.

"I… uh… I told her I had three children," he managed.

"*Three!*" Mother almost laughed. "My! What would she have thought had you told her you actually have five more?"

Hotel guests entered the lobby and crossed in front of them, never realizing the turmoil seated side-by-side.

"Do you love her?"

He finally looked at her. His words carried conviction. "I do not, Marta."

"I feel humiliated and our daughter has witnessed it as well." Mother refused to return his gaze. "How many people here know about your… indiscretion?"

"No one else knows," he answered. "I have told no one."

"I would think your superiors should know," Mother muttered under her breath.

"I swear to you, I am sorry and I will work the rest of my life to make it up to you," he pleaded.

She finally looked at him and raised an eyebrow, "Yes, you will."

And with that, remembering the bundle of letters she still clutched in her hands, she shoved them into his lap and stood. "Letters from your children. The three you admitted to and four of the five others who are living with your wife in an attic in someone else's home."

Father picked up the bundle and stared down at the now wilted flowers tied atop the folded papers. "Vati" was scrawled with care across the front of the first sheet and the sight stabbed him deep in his heart. His guilt was multiplied by each letter he held in his hands.

With a deep sigh, Father stood and followed his wife upstairs to rejoin a hungry, equally deflated Elfriede. After his total war speech earlier in the year, Propaganda Minister Goebbels had closed restaurants in Germany, so the three left the hotel to search for a small market where they were able to use ration cards to purchase some fruit to eat. Mother was in no mood to extend her visit, but agreed to let her husband stay overnight with her and Elfriede and then walk with him to the barracks where they could all say their goodbyes the next day.

It was a long night for Father. Mother had pointedly shown him a small sofa as his bed which made for a rather uncomfortable evening. Sometime during the wee hours of the night, he finally gave up on sleeping and decided to open and read the letters his children had written for him. It was a reminder in black and white of the responsibilities and obligations he had conveniently forgotten during the last few months. He just hoped that he had not thrown away the life he had built for himself before the war.

There is an old adage about a woman scorned and, despite the fact that at first blush Mother appeared to be a pleasant, petite individual, her present fury was something to be feared and Father knew it. So it was the following morning when she and Elfriede walked with Father back to the barracks. He looked overcome with guilt, Elfriede was quiet and withdrawn, but Mother was a woman on a mission.

As they reached the gates of the barracks, Father spotted his superior officer and introduced his wife and daughter to the man a little sheepishly. Small talk ensued and after the pleasantries were complete, an awkward silence fell across the small group.

"Well," Father cleared his throat, still unable to look at his wife and daughter squarely in the eyes, "I must get back to my barracks."

"Auf Wiedersehen," Mother said to him with a slight smile.

Father hesitated, unsure what that smile meant, before wishing Elfriede and Mother a safe trip back to Krumhermsdorf. He walked away, uneasy, leaving his wife standing next to his commander.

"Tell me, sir," Mother asked the man beside her. "What kind of place are you running here? Is it a war or a whorehouse?"

The commander was speechless at the blunt question, but before he could respond, Mother continued by sharing with him the events of the last twenty-four hours. The man may have towered over Mother, but her anger gave her the courage to stand up to him with a single finger wagging in his face. She had the moral high ground and she knew it.

After a few feeble attempts to placate the livid little woman in front of him, the commander lowered his voice so no one walking past them could hear.

"Thank you for bringing this to my attention, Frau Röpke. I promise you I will address the situation."

Mother nodded, somewhat pacified. She and Elfriede picked up their bags and headed for the train station for what would be a long ride back. Mother's mind was spinning. Since Elfriede had been an eyewitness to her father's disgrace, there was no hiding the story from the rest of the children, but Mother could at least keep the details to herself. She steeled herself for their unexpected early arrival to the manor. They would be bombarded with questions and while she would be honest, she thought it best not to be so forthcoming that the present state of her marriage was up for discussion. Years later, long after the war had ended, Mother would actually look back on her adventure in Berlin and laugh while re-telling the story of Father running away with nothing on but his long johns.

For now, the betrayal hurt immensely and the next few weeks would test Marta Röpke in ways she had never been tested before. By August 1944, all theaters were closed by order of Goebbels, Paris had been liberated, and the Soviets were in Poland. Rumors swirled that the war was not progressing the way Hitler had envisioned, and just a few weeks ago Hitler had escaped an assassination attempt. Yet, still he continued headlong toward disaster. It appeared that everyone but Hitler was beginning to accept the reality of the war's outcome.

Word from Bremen had trickled to a rare letter. The Müllers hadn't written in months and I remember crying, concerned that something bad had happened to Uta and Manfred. Mother would reassure me saying they had probably evacuated Bremen and had not had time to write, but I could see that she was putting on a brave face.

The last letter we received from Günter was also several months old. In his last writing, he had told Mother he was still stationed near Bremen, but he no longer shared stories of his duties. His letter also seemed hurried and was much briefer than previous letters had been. Worry was etched across my mother's face.

Perhaps the biggest blow came in August. A church member from Bremen sent Mother a letter relating a particularly devastating bombing on Bremen in the early morning hours of August 18, 1944. The resulting firestorm destroyed 25,000 Bremen homes, killed over 1,000 citizens and left thousands more homeless. One of those who had been killed was Uncle Christian. Many years later, Mother saw a newspaper article and photograph about the bombing, said to be the worst Bremen sustained during the war. She carefully cut the article out, wrote the date of the bombing in ink on one corner of the photo, and added the words, "My brother found under the ashes." She kept that article the rest of her life as a reminder of what she had lost.

But on a quiet day in late August 1944, Mother simply sank onto the sofa in the attic, at first unwilling to grasp the concept that her brother was gone. While she did eventually mourn his loss, she knew she wouldn't be able to travel to Bremen for any type of funeral for her brother. The trip back home was entirely too dangerous. She could do no more than share her loss with all of us in a solemn makeshift ceremony in our attic.

The following day, a telegram was brought to our apartment. Karl-Heinz opened the door and beckoned Mother to sign for the delivery. After signing, Mother held the unread telegram against her heart as she walked to the kitchen table. We all gathered around, knowing full-well the type of news telegrams normally conveyed. Mother was reluctant to glance at the words on the paper, but once seated, she took a deep breath, held the telegram at arm's length in front of her, and began silently reading.

"Mutti," Karl-Heinz ventured to speak, "what does it say?"

Mother didn't answer, but read it again, attempting to absorb the words.

Helga sat Egon in her lap. "Please tell us, Mutti."

Mother put the telegram face down on the table and sighed heavily. "Your Father has been sent to the Eastern Front."

"He'll be fighting the Soviets?" Karl-Heinz's eyes widened.

Nodding, Mother cupped her mouth with her hand. We all sat silently, the older ones understanding the gravity of that order. Composing herself, she reached for the telegram again with both hands and began folding it.

"Yes, I'm afraid so and I… I think this is my fault."

Helga lifted a wriggling Egon off her lap and released him to walk out of the kitchen to follow Waltraut and Inge. "This is NOT your fault."

"Yes, I'm sure it is," Mother said softly. "I talked to his commander. He said he would handle it and now he has. We may never see your father again and it is all my doing."

Elfriede shook her head. "No, Mutti, you cannot blame yourself."

Helga agreed. "This may just be a coincidence. His unit might have been called up anyway."

"Perhaps." Mother turned the idea over in her mind. "I just wish I had never gone to Berlin to see him. Maybe this would not have happened if I had stayed here."

Seldom the voice of reason, Helga suddenly displayed maturity beyond her years. "We may never know why he is going to the front. We can only know that he is and pray for his safety while there."

Mother finally nodded, somewhat consoled by the rational argument her eldest daughter presented.

Yet, in the next breath, Helga provided another argument more in line with the Helga we all knew and loved. "Besides, you're not the guilty party here, *he* is. I think he's probably getting what he deserves!"

"Helga!" Mother said. "I liked your first suggestion much better. Let us all remember to pray that God will look after him."

We had for some time been insulated from the war while in Krumhermsdorf, but events were changing quickly and our place of refuge in eastern Germany now felt isolated and claustrophobic. School attendance had been sketchy at best, but now classes had been dismissed altogether. Correspondence from Günter and other acquaintances in Bremen had stopped completely, Uncle Christian had been killed, and all we knew about Father was that he was somewhere on the Eastern Front. With Soviet troops now in Poland, more refugees passed through the village from the east on their way to Dresden and other larger locales deeper into Germany. With the influx of civilians, Dresden's population was reported to have swollen from 600,000 to over one million. Basic public services were stretched to their limits and resources were strained all over the Third Reich. There would be no more excursions to Dresden for our family.

As the calendar turned to 1945, we were holding on to a tenuous hope for normalcy, but that would be shattered on the night of February 13th. I'm not sure what caught our attention first. I doubt we could have heard the familiar sounds of the first air raid sirens that moaned in Dresden just before 10:00 p.m., but I remember stepping out onto our balcony with the rest of my family and seeing what appeared to be Christmas trees on the horizon over Dresden. It was very beautiful. Twinkling lights slowly floated from the sky to the ground below. But, what I didn't understand in that moment was that those mesmerizing images spelled doom for the beautiful city in the distance. I later learned the mysterious lights I had seen were magnesium parachute flares dropped to light targets for 800 RAF Lancaster bombers.

Just after 10:00 p.m., we heard the drone of the British planes and we stood transfixed on the manor's balcony, watching in horror as bomb after bomb was dropped and explosions rocked the city, turning the horizon into massive clouds of fire billowing toward the bombers themselves. Dresden had no anti-aircraft defenses and so took the brunt of the bombing without a response. Though the bombing seemed to last forever, the raid only lasted twenty minutes or so. It was enough. We had heard that refugees had been content to sleep in the streets, in parks, or wherever they could find because every house, every building was full. Where could all those people go to escape the onslaught? I now know that I was witnessing from afar the death of thousands and the destruction of a city of remarkable cultural significance.

I don't know how long we stood on that balcony staring, weeping, praying that we would wake up from the nightmare we witnessed. Mother finally ushered us back inside and spoke in soothing tones, urging us to seek the relief of sleep in our bedroom. I'm not sure I slept, but as I lay there in the quiet rural night curled beside my sisters in our big bed, my mind reeled at the horror that must be playing out on the streets near the River Elbe, streets I had walked and buildings I had admired. I thought of the zoo we had visited a few months before on our last trip to the city, the *Frauenkirche* services we had attended, and the *Semperoper* filled with music. But most of all, I thought of all the people who had pinned their hope of security on staying in Dresden. The city had been spared until now, but tonight that truce had been broken. Dresden was an inferno.

Sometime after midnight, a second round of bombing began, waking us, urging us back to the balcony, and leaving us speechless. There were twice as many bombers and the hum of their engines filled the distance between us. What could be left of Dresden after the first attack? The city was ablaze and it was hard to imagine there were sections of the city that had not already been incinerated. But flames swirled anew and swept through the city with abandon.

Around 10:30 the next morning, American bombers pummeled what was left of the city and low-flying Mustangs dove, strafing any movement with bullets. The city we had visited and admired not so long ago no longer stood and the death toll had to be astronomical. Having lived through bombings in the past, I thought I was accustomed to the fear of it all, but witnessing the horror in such a panoramic view renewed the sense of terror and helped complete the picture of an overall mission. We were sent to the east for our safety, yet the war had followed us and was now encroaching from all sides: the British and Americans from the west, the Polish and Soviets from the east. Our days in Krumhermsdorf were numbered, but we had no idea where we would need to go to stay out of harm's way. Mother would have to make this decision alone and, like the evacuees who had staked their lives on Dresden as a haven, our lives depended on making the right choice.

For some time after Dresden's demise, we were advised no one should be outside. The zoo had suffered extensive damage, and what animals hadn't died during the bombing or been killed afterward to end their suffering were now on the loose in the surrounding countryside. Until all animals had been accounted for, citizens were told to remain indoors. I had thought only about the people who had lost their lives and the landmarks that no longer stood, but it had never occurred to me that the animals had shared the same fate as the rest of the city. The exotic zoo was no more.

Saxony's proximity to Poland and Czechoslovakia had at one time been our saving grace. It was now a liability. Word trickled in to the village that the Polish and Soviet Armies were on the move and their most imminent objectives were to free Prague from the Nazis and take over eastern Germany. Worse gossip had preceded the Soviet Red Army and carried tales of rapes, murder, and brutality that followed in its wake. We were only 100 miles from Prague. Our rural setting could protect us no longer.

Early one evening at the end of March, we were all seated around the kitchen table talking when the *Bürgermeister* paid a visit to our attic home. He greeted us all with his usual charisma, but it was evident his mind was occupied with more serious thoughts.

"May I speak to you, Frau Röpke?"

Mother nodded and asked us all to go to our bedroom while they spoke. Unlike the visit from Colonel Pfiffer to discuss Helga, we weren't able to overhear any of the conversation between Mother and the *Bürgermeister* no matter how hard we tried. Their hushed tones were a testament to the serious topic between them and the visit seemed to last forever. But only a moment after we heard him leave, Mother opened the bedroom door and asked us all to gather around the kitchen table.

We were all speaking at once, anxious to hear what the mayor had shared. Mother stood at one end of the table and raised her hand in the air, signaling for quiet.

"I need you all to listen to me very carefully," she said as she looked at each one of us. "We are going home."

"To Bremen?" Helga breathed excitedly. "When do we need to start packing? When do we leave?"

"We will only be taking our identification papers and what we are wearing," Mother answered.

"What about our furniture?" Karl-Heinz looked around at the familiar pieces. "Will they be shipped later?"

"What about our big bed that Vati built?" I chimed in.

Elfriede interrupted the barrage of questions. "Mutti, what did the *Bürgermeister* tell you?"

Mother hesitated, unsure if she should shield her children from the realities of the danger ahead. Helga was fourteen, I was now nine, and Egon had just turned four. We had been through a lot as a family and we needed to know the truth; we needed to know what we were facing.

"He said the Red Army would be here soon and… and he said… he said if we want to get out alive, we had to leave here… *tonight.*"

Marta, exact age unknown.
Bremen, Germany, early 1900s.

Marie Dreyer and Ludwig Koelling (far right), parents of Marta Koelling Röpke. Bremen, Germany, 1933.

Marta at age 18.
Bremen, Germany, 1918.

Diedrech "Dirk" Heinrich Herman Röpke. Bremen, Germany, circa 1935.

An early Röpke family photo. Back L-R: Dirk, Marta, Giesela; Front L-R: Elfrieda, Karl-Heinz and Helga (Günter not pictured). Bremen, Germany, circa 1934-35.

Dirk Röpke.
Bremen, Germany, circa 1936.

Giesela Röpke (age 2) with a nurse in Bremen, Germany. Marta wrote the date across the back of this picture: May 17, 1936. Giesela would die several months later.

The Röpke family at home in Bremen, Germany. (L-R) Karl-Heinz, Marta, Edith, Helga, Giesela, Elfrieda, circa 1936 (Dirk and Günter are not pictured).

*Marta and Dirk,
location unknown, circa 1940.*

RAF Vickers-Wellington Bomber crash site at Delmenhorst (near Bremen). On nickel raid (dropping leaflets over Germany), the plane was hit by anti-aircraft flak and crashed in flames on Easter Morning, March 24, 1940. Both pilots died (one in the crash, the other a week later from his burns); four other aircrew captured and sent to POW camps in Germany and Poland. Photo taken by unknown photographer, March 24, 1940. Röpke family collection.

Marta and her children: Back L-R: Elfrieda, Inge, Waltraut, and Günter; Front L-R: Karl-Heinz, Egon (seated), Marta, Edith, and Helga. Bremen, Germany, 1941.

Manor in Krumhermsdorf, Saxony near Dresden where the Röpke family resided from 1943-1945. Picture taken by Karl-Heinz Röpke in early 1980s.

Vor 30 Jahren: Der Westen sank in Schutt und Asche

Zum 30. Mai jährt sich an diesem Wochenende der düstere Tag in der jüngeren Bremer Geschichte, an der Nacht vom 18. auf den 19. August 1944 legte ein Bombenhagel den Bremer Westen in Schutt und Asche. Nur etwa eine halbe Stunde lang flogen rund 500 britische Bomber gezielte Angriffe auf die Hansestadt. Das Ergebnis des Flächenbombardements war grauenhaft. Unter berstenden Mauern und in einem Feuersturm unvorstellbaren Ausmaßes starben 1058 Männer, Frauen und Kinder. Als die Sirenen Entwarnung heulten, waren 25 000 Wohnungen vernichtet und 49 100 Menschen obdachlos. Eine einzige Nacht hatte genügt, um den Bremer Westen auszulöschen.

Der Angriff in der Nacht vom 18. auf den 19. August 1944 war nicht der erste, den Bremen im Zweiten Weltkrieg erlebte. Bereits 131mal zuvor hatten in den fünf Kriegsjahren die Sirenen der Hansestadt Alarm gegeben. Doch meist galten die Bombardements alliierter Bomber bis dahin vorwiegend militärischen Zielen. Dem Hafen beispielsweise, den Werften oder Stadtvierteln, in denen man Unterkommen der Rüstungsindustrie vermutete.

Die Bremer hatten längst gelernt, mit Bomben und Dunkern zu leben. Doch als sie am 18. August, spätabends in die Keller flüchteten, ahnte niemand, welch ein Inferno wenig später über die Stadt hereinbrechen würde.

Kurz nach 22 Uhr an einem brütend heißen Sommerabend war in der Hansestadt Fliegeralarm gegeben worden. Über Helgoland hatten deutsche Abwehrstellen Bomberverbände ausgemacht. Doch noch zwei Stunden dauerte die Ungewißheit, ob der Angriff Bremen oder — wie so oft zuvor — Zielen im Binnenland gelten würde.

Nach genau 23 Uhr glaubten die Menschen in den Kellern, wieder einmal davongekommen zu sein. Über der Stadt hörten sie das Brummen von Flugzeugmotoren, ohne daß etwas geschah. Doch die Entwarnung blieb aus. Über Helgoland flogen immer neue Bomberpulks heran. Als die Armada mit der todbringenden Last über Cuxhaven nach Süden abdrehte, wurden die Befürchtungen deutscher Beobachtungsposten fast zur Gewißheit: Bremen ist in Gefahr.

Drei Minuten vor Mitternacht hat die erste Welle der Kampfverbände die Hansestadt erreicht. Was folgt, ist in der Kriegsgeschichte Bremens ohne Beispiel. Pausenlos decken die Maschinen die unter ihnen liegenden Straßenzüge und Stadtteile mit Bombenteppichen ein. Dicht bei dicht fallen Sprengkörper und Brandsätze. Vergeblich versucht die Flak die Angriffe abzuwehren. Störgeräte und abgeworfene Stanniolstreifen machen die Ortungsapparaturen der deutschen Abwehr hilflos.

Nur 35 Minuten später, um 0.36 Uhr, drehen die Bombergeschwader ab. Unter ihnen brennt Bremen. Vergeblich versuchen Feuerwehren und Luftschutzabteilungen einen von Phosphorbomben entfachten Brand ganzer Straßenzüge einzudämmen. Vielen Bremern, die zu früh aus den Kellern kamen, wird dieser Feuersturm zum Verhängnis.

Erst in den Morgenstunden des 19. August läßt sich das wahre Ausmaß der Schreckensnacht absehen. Bremen ist eine trostlos zerstörte Stadt. Im Gebiet zwischen der Weserstraße im Osten, dem Waller Ring im Westen, der Weser im Süden und der Eisenbahnlinie Bremen—Bremerhaven im Norden, steht kaum noch ein Stein auf dem anderen.

Allenfalls ragen rußgeschwärzte Ruinen hier und dort in die Höhe.

Und das Oberkommando der Wehrmacht verschweigt den Umfang der Katastrophe. Zynisch läßt die deutsche Heeresführung über Rundfunk verbreiten: „In der Nacht war Bremen das Ziel eines britischen Terrorangriffs. Es entstanden Gebäudeschäden und Personenverluste." Kein Wort über die Zahl der Toten, keine Angaben über das Schicksal von 49 100 Menschen, die in einer einzigen Nacht alles verloren.

Auch heute — 30 Jahre nach der Katastrophe — ist immer noch nicht genau bekannt, welche Bombenlast in jener Augustnacht über Bremen niederging. Schätzungen gehen davon aus, daß es rund 130 000 bis 140 000 Luftminen und Sprengbomben sowie 120 000 Brandbomben waren, die den Bremer Westen vernichteten. Alles in allem Munition mit einem Gewicht von mehreren Millionen Kilogramm.

Noch Tage nach dem Angriff spielen sich in Bremen erschütternde Szenen ab. Vergeblich versuchen Menschen unter den Toten ihre vermißten Angehörigen zu finden. Nur bei 683 Opfern gelingt die Identifizierung. Die übrigen sind bis zur Unkenntlichkeit verbrannt. Im Lesmona-Keller an Panzenberg, einer alten Zigarettenfabrik, machten Bergungstrupps die grauenhafteste Entdeckung. Zusammengesunken finden sie 185 Tote. Alle waren erstickt, als neben ihrem Unterschlupf ein Kohlenlager Feuer fing und giftige Gase auch in den Keller eindrangen.

30 Jahre später sind die Spuren des Dramas vernarbt. Einzig auf dem Osterholzer Friedhof finden sich noch Hinweise auf die Nacht des 18./19. August 1944: Die Massengräber der Opfer.

Unknown German newspaper (printed years later) detailing 1944 bombing that killed Marta's brother. In the bottom left margin of the clipping a note was found in Marta's handwriting: "My brother found under the ashes."

"We are going to Bremen;
you can find something better than death everywhere."

-The Town Musicians of Bremen, The Brothers Grimm

EIGHT
ESCAPING THE EAST
LATE MARCH 1945

While we each got dressed, topping off each outfit with coats, scarves, and shoes, I noticed Mother tearing the lining from her suit jacket. She hurriedly grabbed all our identification papers, ration cards, and several family photographs and began placing them evenly between the linen jacket material and the torn liner. With a swift hand, she stitched the lining back in place and then shrugged into the jacket, smoothing it over her blouse and skirt.

Glancing around at each one of us, Mother nodded, satisfied we had enough layers of clothing for the trip. She asked Karl-Heinz to get the stroller. For a pedestrian-reliant family, that stroller still came in handy for tired little legs. And even though Egon and Inge were now four and five years old respectively, Mother knew the stroller would help expedite the long journey we were about to take. Helga and Elfriede gathered what they could in the way of foodstuffs from the kitchen and stowed them away in a few small bags while Waltraut and I saw that Inge and Egon were buttoned up against the cool night.

We stood in the kitchen looking around at the attic apartment that had been our home for the past year-and-a-half. In this grand manor we had lived and grown; we had used this as our base from which we explored Dresden and escaped the war, if only for a time. The Colonel had arrived home just yesterday, as stern and unapproachable as ever, and immediately began preparations downstairs to move his wife, son, and furnishings from the Manor. While we were fearful of being captured by the Red Army, it must have been nothing to the fear Colonel Pfiffer felt. The Soviets would consider it quite a prize to meet up with a German officer.

Our big bed, the sofa, chairs, *schrank*, and kitchen table were all being left behind. We had shipped them from Bremen and they had served us well, but now we had no option but to leave them behind. While I understood they were only wood, glue, and nails, it was still emotional leaving without those familiar pieces. They were ours; Father had labored over each one. How could we just walk away from them? I was reluctant to give them up, but Mother reminded me that Father could always build new furniture, but our family could not be replaced.

"Children," Mother held Egon's hand and looked at each one of us as she spoke from the heart, "the *Bürgermeister* told me the Soviets will soon be here. He said the safest thing we can do is to try to get back to west Germany where the Americans and British are, where our home is, and we must not tarry. I don't know where your father and Günter are, but I pray that after the war they will find us, and home is where they will look first. *Our* house is gone, but I hope my parents' house is still standing so we will have a place to live. I don't know what we will encounter as we try to get back to Bremen, but it is a long trip and it may be very dangerous, so we must stay together, stay close, and be very careful. We will travel by train as far as we can, but there is a lot of damage from the war, so we may have to do a lot of walking."

It was quiet in the room as we all absorbed her words.

"I'm scared, Mutti," I finally admitted to Mother.

Mother's eyes appeared misty, but she blinked rapidly and looked at me with honesty. "I am too, Edith. We are all scared. That's why it is important that we stay together."

She glanced at Karl-Heinz who nodded in support. She took a deep breath. "I want everyone to hold hands."

We all stood in a tight circle and took hold of the hand next to us with Mother completing the circle. "We are going to pray to God that He will be with us and will be with Günter and your father, too."

As we all bowed our heads, Mother quietly voiced a prayer. As she spoke, Elfriede sniffled and a tear trickled down Helga's face. We were all nervous; even the little ones knew we were about to embark on something treacherous. Mother ended with an "Amen" which was immediately echoed by each of us, then we turned to leave the attic for the train station in the village.

Service was still available to Neustadt, so we boarded the next train, content to ride the rails as far as possible. The train car was packed, but we managed to find seats near one another. I sat with Karl-Heinz and Inge in the seat in front of Mother, Egon, and Waltraut; Helga and Elfriede slid into a seat across the aisle from Mother. I looked around at the people near us. Everyone was on edge, their faces etched with worry. Elderly couples clutched their bags, mothers held their children's hands, and youngsters sat stiffly, alert and aware. Conversations were serious and discreet; we were all absorbed in our own private plans.

The night slid by as we churned farther and farther away from Saxony. But were we escaping quickly enough? For as long as I could remember, we had watched the skies, terrified of the death and destruction that might fall from on high, but now a new fear was pervading our thoughts—tanks and infantry and soldiers. Troops were now on the ground in our homeland and we could only hope that we could evade capture or worse.

The railway was still intact beyond Neustadt, but as we neared Dresden we knew it was only a matter of time before we would have to leave the relative comfort of the train and begin walking. We had been eyewitnesses to the crippling siege on the city just weeks before. Rail service could not have withstood the onslaught. As if on cue, the train slowed, traveling for some time near a crawl. Many of the adults murmured to one another.

Helga leaned out of her seat across the aisle toward Mother and asked in a low voice, "What is happening, Mutti?"

"Everyone thinks we're several miles south of Dresden and I'm sure the rails are badly damaged. We'll just stay on as long as we can," Mother said as she shifted a sleepy Egon in her arms.

Karl-Heinz turned around and faced the rest of the family. "I don't mind walking, Mutti, but how will we know how to get home?"

Mother looked around at the seven faces staring back at her. "I don't know, son. We'll follow what signs we can find. We'll follow people. We'll just head northwest."

After some time, the train finally steamed to a stop and we stood, looking down at the seats and underneath to make sure we had the stroller and our packages of food. We stood in line in the aisle, filing out of the train car with the rest of the travelers, down the steps onto the graveled rail bed. We were not near a platform, but in the middle of pastureland, somewhere near Dresden with nothing but the night sky to guide our steps.

"Take hands!" Mother reminded us as we walked in a tightly formed little procession from the train. Once we had walked several steps away from the rails, she stopped, regrouping, making sure she had us all around her. "Do *not* move away from each other. We stay together."

We all voiced our agreement and, reassured we were heeding her warning, Mother began trodding across the pasture, at an angle from the train.

"Why don't we follow the tracks?" Helga asked, watching various groups of people walking in different directions from the train.

"We need to head away from Dresden," Mother reasoned. "If that's north to Dresden" she pointed in the direction of the double lines of steel "then we need to be heading in this direction—to the northwest."

"Why don't we go to Berlin?" Elfriede asked, kicking a small stone away.

"Berlin is the last place we need to go," Mother said as she paused to lift Egon into the stroller and let Helga push it across the bumpy ground. "Hitler will be in Berlin and that's where the Allied armies will go to find him. Berlin will be one of the most dangerous places to be right now. As a matter of fact, I think we are safer if we stay away from large cities."

"Ow!" I yelped as a low bush slapped against my leg.

"Shhh!" Helga turned her head to silence me as she trudged forward.

"I can't see where I'm stepping," Elfriede grumbled.

"Be very careful. I don't want anyone hurt, but we need to keep going as long as we can tonight, children." Mother took Inge's hand. "Later we'll find some place to stop for the night."

Her voice was firm and we knew that meant there was no use pleading our cause. Besides, we weren't alone. There were a few other couples and families walking just in front of us, and having others nearby must have given Mother the motivation to continue moving forward. Thankfully, the moon peeked from behind clouds from time to time, making it easier to watch our steps, but as the evening wore on, the night air became cooler. I tugged my coat collar up around my chin and tightened the scarf I was wearing in a constant battle between cool air hitting my throat and exertion warming me up under the layers of clothes. One minute I was shivering, the next minute I was fanning my reddened nose and cheeks.

We had no idea what time it was. Mother had a watch, but it wasn't working. The dainty gold timepiece had been losing time lately and there had been no way to have it repaired. Even though it was now more decorative than functional, she continued to wear it because Father had given it to her years before. I was glad she kept it. We had precious few tangible items of sentimental value anymore. So, heedless of the hour, we marched on in the rural countryside, knowing only that it must be after midnight and comforted that we weren't alone on our trek.

An elderly couple from the train had been traveling with our unofficial group for some time, but they had not been able to keep the same pace as our family and the others around us, and their "bones just wouldn't hold up" as well as ours. So, they stopped to rest for the night in a wooded area as the rest of us continued on.

I heard Karl-Heinz whisper to Mother, "Shouldn't we stay with them?"

Mother shook her head sadly. "I would love to help them, but I'm responsible for you and your brother and sisters. We have to keep going, Karl-Heinz. Our lives may depend on it."

He nodded, understanding, and glanced back at me. My brother didn't have to say a word to me—I knew what he was thinking. Could *I* make it? I met his gaze and nodded to reassure him. I could. I could because my brother was with me. I could because my mother was determined that we all make it.

An hour or so later, as we were picking our way around bushes and trees, we heard the low drone of vehicles coming closer on a nearby road. The family of four in front of us fell to the ground and motioned for us to do the same.

"Down!" Mother whispered as loudly as possible. Instantly we all flattened ourselves against the hard ground, or hid by trees or bushes, whatever was closest.

Helga quickly grabbed Egon from the stroller, knelt down behind a fencepost swallowed by shrubbery, and tipped the stroller on its side.

We lay motionless, heads down, barely breathing for fear our intake of breath would be heard despite the fact that the motors bearing down on us were significantly louder. I motioned to Inge with a finger across my lips and she nodded, knowing the importance of being quiet.

All eyes scanned the roadway ahead. We heard gears shifting in an attempt to navigate the rutted road, but there were no beams of light to signal their approach. Suddenly, two vehicles shot out of the woods and into the lane. We could make out a pair of men in each and could tell they were in uniform, but it was difficult to see their features with the moon tucked behind a bank of clouds. Were they German? It was hard to tell in the darkness. And though we couldn't clearly grasp their words, we did catch the tone and cadence of their voices. My heart stopped beating for a moment as Karl-Heinz slowly turned his head to look at me. We knew those accents. Karl-Heinz and Michael used those same accents in play many times at Krumhermsdorf Manor. The men were Russian.

Thankfully, we blended in among the bushes and weeds beyond the fencerow and the Russians drove on into the night without slowing down. Like statues, we continued to lay still long after they had passed us, unwilling to move lest the military vehicles returned to shine their lights on us. Finally satisfied we were alone, we got to our feet and began moving again.

I have no way of knowing how far we walked that first night. Mother insisted we keep up with the group of people with us and they didn't stop for what I'm sure was hours into the early morning. Eventually, we found a grove of trees and decided it would make a good secluded place to rest. Sure my feet were incapable of scooting one more mile, I finally collapsed on the hard ground under the trees. The exhaustion kept the worries at bay and allowed me to sleep soundly.

A few hours later, a streak of muted light bent past the tree limbs overhead and woke me. I stretched and my hand hit Elfriede's shoe. I slowly blinked, finally remembering where I was. As I sat up, I saw that Mother had already risen and was taking inventory of the modest amount of food taken from the Manor the night before. Helga and Elfriede sat up as well and I nudged Karl-Heinz awake to join us. Mother woke the little ones and doled out a measured amount of fruit for each of us.

"We all need to eat," Mother explained, particularly to my youngest siblings. "I don't know when we'll find more food, so I'm going to try to make what we brought with us last as long as possible. Do you all understand?"

Egon nodded enthusiastically, happy to be munching on anything at the moment.

The other people around us began gathering what they had brought for the trip, and were soon heading out of the grove. Mother motioned for us to do the same and within minutes our ragtag group's trek was underway once more under the early morning sky. Several hours later, we came across a small stream and stopped, excited to have water to drink. We each knelt and scooped the water in cupped hands. It was cold and I remember thinking water had never tasted as good, never as refreshing. Mother lamented the fact we couldn't store the water, but hoped we would be fortunate enough to find other fresh streams on our way home.

As the day wore on, our numbers grew. Refugees, homeless, and injured were all taking to the open countryside, hoping only to flee the effects of the war. There was, I thought, a certain comfort in being surrounded by others similar to us, but by now it had been ingrained in us not to trust anyone for fear of reprisals. So, we walked on, sharing only an occasional pleasantry with those around us; saving our energy for the journey, for pressing on.

"Edith," Karl-Heinz nudged me at one point. "Look."

He pointed northward in the heavens and I squinted against the sun, not knowing what I would find. It didn't take long to see what had caught his eye. High-flying formations of planes flew overhead. Their contrails streamed behind them, striping the blue sky with lines of white. It was chilling. They carried death in their underbellies and I prayed for the people who would have to seek shelter from their wrath. Mother had followed our gazes and had seen the bombers, too.

"Mutti, where do you think they are headed?" I asked her.

We had no map; we only generally knew where we were or how far we had traveled, but Mother felt sure we were southwest of Dresden and she knew what lay a couple of hours north.

"What city is in that direction?" I pressed.

Mother looked tired and sad, but finally answered me. "Berlin."

I cringed. If a city like Dresden could be dealt a severe blow at the hands of the Allies, how much more would Berlin suffer? It was, after all, our capital. From the Reich Chancellery, Hitler dispensed his plans. Bremen might have been a target earlier in the war, but Berlin must be the ultimate target, the ultimate end. I wiped away a tear. I just wanted this war to end. I didn't understand the conquest of surrounding countries; I didn't understand

Hitler's need for power. I just wanted to go home and I wanted my family back together—including Father and Günter. I prayed that would happen.

The eight of us took small bites of the food we had left, but after noon on the next day our provisions were already running low. It had been drizzling rain all that day and by the time the sun was sinking, our shoes were caked with mud, we were tired and dirty and more than ready to bed down for the night. After separating from the larger group, our family and a few other individuals found an abandoned barn to call home for the night. Many of the wood planks had either rotted or simply fallen off the walls over time and the roof was missing in several places, but it was, at least, shelter. While we each tried to find dry places under the drafty roof to claim as our own, Helga and Elfriede rearranged fallen leaves in one corner of the old barn to make "beds." But, before settling in for the night, Mother and I worked to scrape the mud from everyone's shoes and Karl-Heinz went scouting outside to find something, anything edible.

"I'm hungry," four-year-old Egon whined.

"I know," Mother consoled him. "But your brother is looking for something. Now, why don't you try to get comfortable in the meantime?"

Waltraut, Inge, and Egon huddled together while Mother and I rubbed their legs with our hands, warming them. The wind whistled in between two crooked boards across from us, a fine mist of precipitation following in its wake. It would, I was sure, be a long, uncomfortable night.

"Look what I found!" Karl-Heinz said as he burst in from outside, wet from the rain that we now heard peppering the roof. Helga and Elfriede joined in our little circle as we watched Karl-Heinz's pleased expression. Holding his coat like a large pouch against his chest, he dropped to his knees in front of us, laid his coat down and slowly peeled back the edges to reveal his surprise in the middle – dozens of plump berries.

"Oooh!" Inge's familiar exclamation came amidst our laughter.

"Is that all you can ever say about anything?" Helga teased.

We laughed, happy to know we would have something to fill our stomachs before morning. Thankfully, the other people in the barn had found their own provisions, so we didn't have to share outside our family. Mother doled out the "meal" to each of us and told us to eat slowly, to enjoy every last bite of our improvised feast. We were glad to oblige. Not only were the berries delicious, but the juice made up for the fact we had nothing to drink that evening.

Each morning we stayed away from major roads and cities, but we were beginning to see a common theme in every village and town through which we traveled: there would be massive rebuilding to do after the war. Each village was damaged heavily, houses were gone, lives lost, and millions displaced. And as we walked westward, the number of refugees joining us increased. The masses were becoming more diverse as well, as German civilians were now joined by wounded German soldiers simply abandoning a losing cause. Each of us, though, had a commonality: we were in a desperate march to escape the inevitable takeover in the east by the Soviets.

I'm not sure if walking with great numbers of people slowed our progress or motivated us to walk longer and farther, but two weeks after leaving Krumhermsdorf, we had at least made some headway in reducing the 500 miles we had to go to get home. We were tired, caked in a thin film of dried mud, and hungry. We might have been one-third of the way home when we and several hundred other people made our way into another nameless town which had suffered under the onslaught of the Allied offensive.

The few shopowners who were still open for business eyed us suspiciously. What little produce they still had to sell was meant for their own residents, so they didn't like the throngs of refugees passing through. It was obvious none of us were in a position to walk into their establishments and purchase anything. We were on our last legs, desperate for food, shelter, and clothing. Those shopowners, no doubt, had to watch the masses warily for thieves and shoplifters in order to maintain what little inventory they had left. Unfortunately, war had made even the meekest of us hopeless enough to take from them in order to survive.

Despite their harsh glares, Mother knew we all needed a few minutes to rest, so when we reached the town center, she told us all to find a place to sit. Elfriede had been pushing Inge in the stroller and was happy to find a shady tree under which to park Inge, while she leaned against the tree's trunk. Helga and Waltraut sank down on the ground near Elfriede. Mother, Egon, Karl-Heinz, and I eased down onto the dusty cobblestone street.

I sat, mesmerized at the sheer volume of people moving past us in a constant flow through the village. While most people were on foot, from time to time a farmer would pass by with a horse-drawn cart piled high with furniture and family, threading his way through the pedestrians.

Without warning, we heard the gunning of engines and before we could react, a circle of large trucks and armored cars had entered the city center. Men in brown uniforms jumped from their vehicles onto the street with their guns in hand.

Mother moved nearer to us, "Stay close, children."

My heart was in my throat and without realizing it, I was clutching Karl-Heinz's arm with a death grip. Long before any of the commanders spoke to the stunned crowd facing them, I knew who they were.

Several men wielding guns shouted at the crowd, motioning toward a building down the street. Moments later, one of the soldiers stepped onto an armored vehicle to be better heard by the citizens and refugees. He lifted his gun into the sky for silence and, with everyone's attention fixed on him, he spoke loudly in fluent German, *"People! Move into the building on the corner of the street! You are now prisoners of the Soviet Red Army!"*

NINE
PRISONERS OF WAR
LATE MARCH 1945

Unsure how to react, I looked at Mother, who stood up and motioned for Elfriede to lift Inge back into the stroller. She silently lifted her hand, signaling us to stand and hold hands as we were herded with hundreds of other German refugees down the street. Without her voicing the commands, I knew the drill by now—stay close together, don't speak. Fear has a way of reinforcing learned behaviors and heightening the importance of self-control. I was treading lightly, not looking at our captors; I was being quiet and compliant. We all were.

Armed Soviets barked orders at us in their native language. Though I didn't understand what they were saying, there was no mistaking the urgency of the commands. In mass, we shuffled along a dusty, damaged street to a large building with double doors. Though it had some damage to one side of the roof, the majority of the building looked relatively unscathed. I stumbled at the doorway, blinded from the sunlit avenue as we entered the darkened interior. It was a cavernous space with a wooden floor. Our shoes clicked against the hard surface as we circled the interior, making room for the hundreds behind us who were told to get inside.

Mother held Egon and was followed by Elfriede who was pushing Inge in the stroller while the rest of were close on their heels. As frightened as I was, I remember focusing instead on how much Elfriede's chore had just been lightened: for suddenly the stroller's wheels rolled effortlessly across the hard floor, a stark difference from the bumpy ride Inge and Egon had endured since leaving Krumhermsdorf. Maybe I was grasping at something, anything, positive to think about, but I remember being glad that Elfriede could push that stroller so easily for the time being.

"Move! Move! Line up against the walls," the Russian who spoke German yelled.

Mother's eyes darted back to us. I could see an undescribed emotion there, but I didn't want to examine it too closely. Instead, we all continued moving around the room until the last individuals trickled in from outside.

"Sit!"

Unanimously we did so. Sandwiched between Inge, Helga, and Karl-Heinz, I tucked my legs underneath me, but this was one time we wouldn't be pushing and shoving our siblings away. Their nearness was actually comforting and I took a deep breath to calm my shaking hands. I have no idea how many people were packed into that big room, but there were easily hundreds and we were all sitting on the floor against the walls, facing our guards, stunned that we were now prisoners of war. As good as it felt to be sitting with a roof over our heads, I would have given anything at that moment to be out on the open road, heading home to Bremen.

One of the officers circled his hand over his head, yelling something in Russian to several soldiers. They immediately scrambled, their boots thumping as they went around the room, slamming three sets of metal doors. The sound was deafening in the large space and was more so because there was so little noise from the occupants to distract from the closing of those exits. I heard a few children whimpering, but the adults did their best to soothe them. Our imaginations were running wild wondering what their intentions were, but there was no explanation given. Instead, two or three guards stood at each exit while a half-dozen or so soldiers milled around, talking and laughing, totally ignoring their prisoners.

We sat quietly, not sure if we were allowed to talk, but it gave me time to study our fellow captives. It was a diverse group spanning all ages. Some were healthy, some injured, some old, some young, but all unkempt, tired and defeated. Next to Mother was a woman with two sons: one was a teenager—maybe fourteen or fifteen—and the younger son looked to be about twelve—the same age as Karl-Heinz. On the other side of that family were two German soldiers. Their uniforms were not only extremely dirty, but no longer fit their frames testifying to how long they had gone without a proper meal. They both looked exhausted, their eyes underscored by dark circles of fatigue, but to make matters worse, one of the two had crutches propped up behind him against the wall. His pant leg was ripped, revealing a heavily bandaged leg he extended in front of him.

I wanted so badly to ask them if they had been on the Eastern Front. Perhaps they had seen my father. But I was old enough to realize that was highly unlikely.

Hours went by. Our captors ignored the few tentative conversations that began in the crowd, so while there was almost a reverent volume in the building, at least people felt free to speak to those around them. Incredibly, Mother was stunned to learn that the woman and her two sons sitting near us were also trying to reach Bremen. It was like finding a long lost relative, and the two women were glad to have found a common kinship.

"Children," Mother turned to us. "I want to introduce you to Frau Meier and her sons."

One by one, she gave our names and ages to the Meier family and I smiled, sure their heads were spinning if they were trying to remember each of us.

"Frau Meier and her sons are also from Bremen." Mother beamed. "This is Erich, her oldest and this is Hans, her youngest. Karl-Heinz, you and Hans are the same age."

We all nodded, acknowledging the introduction and Karl-Heinz moved closer to Hans and Erich. While the three boys said little to each other initially, I knew Karl-Heinz was glad to have someone his age to talk to besides his sisters.

"Excuse me," the healthy German soldier leaned away from the wall and glanced over at Mother. "Did I hear you say your families are from Bremen?"

Mother was reluctant to talk to the man, so she was guarded in her response. "Yes, we have been living in Saxony and we were leaving the east on our way back home."

The man introduced himself as Max and his injured companion as Ernst, and explained that they were from Hannover, just 122 km (75 miles) from Bremen. Fate, it seemed, had placed us all together; we were all headed in the same direction.

Less cautious than my mother, Frau Meier turned to the German soldier and whispered the question uppermost in our minds, "What do you think they are going to do with us?"

Peering up at the soldiers brandishing their weapons not far from us, Max looked back at Mother and Frau Meier, then glanced at each one of their children before answering. He slowly shook his head and, not wanting the younger ones to hear, kept his voice low.

"For me and Ernst… I'm sure they will want to take us back to Russia as prisoners. But, for your families… maybe they just want to keep you in eastern Germany where you will be under their control after the war."

Frau Meier agreed. "Yes, I'm sure they just want to prevent us from going home."

Throwing her normal cautious nature aside, Mother tossed out her own opinion. "Maybe, but I've heard too many stories about the Red Army and what they have done to women and…."

Mother's voice trailed off as she choked back her deep concern, concern for our safety and her own. She took a deep breath before continuing, "I don't have to remind you we are German, and the Soviets will not have forgotten that our troops crossed into *their* country uninvited."

Max and Ernst agreed, leaving Frau Meier shaken, and Mother pondering what few options she had should someone try to take her or one of her daughters. For years, Mother had been wary of trusting anyone, but faced with the Red Army in front of her and two German soldiers beside her, she had little choice but to trust the two men who were her countrymen. Although, as she glanced at Ernst's injured leg, she doubted the soldiers' effectiveness against the armed Russians pacing nearby.

As if to reinforce her sense of helplessness, Ernst winced as he tried to move his leg and Mother could see fresh blood seeping through the bandages. With no supplies available and certain the Soviets would have no sympathy for their injured enemy, Mother slid closer to him.

"May I take a look at the wound?" she asked.

He looked unsure, but Mother waved away his objections. "I'm certainly not a medical professional, but I have had plenty of experience dressing wounds while raising eight children."

Satisfied, he leaned back and let Mother gingerly unwrap the bandage from around his leg. The wound on one side of his left calf muscle appeared to extend to his shin bone. It was deep, but at least it didn't appear to be infected. There was no way to clean the wound and there was no clean fabric available to replace the soiled bandages she had just removed. Ernst insisted the Soviets not be asked for a medic or any medication, so Mother had little choice but to rewrap the wound with the old bandage. She did so more neatly and tightly in an attempt to stem the flow of blood.

Ernst was grateful for her handiwork and told her so, but she worried about his injury. He was several years older than Günter and that thought made her extremely emotional. If Ernst's injury continued to go untreated, it could become much more serious than it already was. He was young, but he could lose a leg. What if Günter were in the same condition somewhere? Would someone be near him to help? She hadn't heard from him in months and had no idea where he was. She choked back emotion and refused to shed tears. She had to get her younger children home and then, and only then, could she focus on finding her oldest son and her husband. She just prayed they were still alive.

I was not privy to the private discussions the adults had been having a few yards from me. Instead, I had been staring at the walls and memorizing the wooden slats on the floor. I was bored, yet thankful there was nothing of more importance happening to us at the moment. Inge and Egon had fallen asleep, blissfully unaware of the potential danger they were in, and all the while my stomach rumbled with Helga's trying to match it in volume.

The sun had moved lower into the sky, so it must have been late afternoon when we were startled by the banging of the main double doors opening, hitting hard against the wall.

"Up! Get ready to walk!" the German-speaking soldier shouted.

With stiff backs and knees, everyone did their best to hurry to a standing position. Max helped Ernst up as Hans and Karl-Heinz brought his crutches to him. Elfriede took Waltraut's hand in hers and I helped Inge up. Frau Meier assisted Mother as she put Egon in the stroller for Helga to push, but Erich Meier soon stood by Helga's side. The tall, lanky, blond-haired Erich looked at Helga with crystal blue eyes and crooked a brilliant white smile her way.

"I can do that," he offered as his hand smoothed his parted hair to one side. Helga, so surprised she was at a loss for words, finally relented and stepped to one side as Erich took the stroller in hand.

Obviously awed at the teenage boy beside her, Helga finally found her voice. *"Danke."*

She looked up thankfully at Erich with a slight smile and blinked rather demurely. Helga actually looked shy... *Shy!*

Gaping at her, I mouthed silently to her, "Did you just thank him?" I was sure that Erich must be able to see through this award-winning performance from my oldest sister.

She turned her head so Erich couldn't see her face and mouthed to me in response: "Be. Quiet."

She quickly focused once more on Erich and said something to him in a quiet voice that made them both laugh. I rolled my eyes. The joke was on Helga. She was flirting outrageously with Erich, but if she had been able to see her disheveled reflection in a mirror she would have been horrified!

The moment of levity was interrupted by a German command yelled out with a decided Russian accent. "Outside. Stay in line!"

His order was followed by a string of Russian words that no one seemed to grasp. Was it expletives? I'm sure some in the crowd understood Russian, but I wasn't one of them.

Were we being released? Were we being taken outside to be shot? My legs shook; I wasn't sure if it was from terror, hunger, or both. Slowly, we filed through the main doors into the street beyond and the cool early evening air. I inhaled the fresh air and was immediately struck by the smell of… broth.

"They are feeding us!" Karl-Heinz turned his head and said to me quietly.

I couldn't believe it. We were not being freed, but at least they had the decency to see that we didn't starve to death either. We were each handed two metal cups—one smaller than the other—and then told to stand in line around the building, slowly making our way to a long row of makeshift tables. As we approached the servers, we copied the person in front of us by extending our cups—the smaller was filled with water; the larger was filled with warm broth. Another soldier motioned for us to keep moving toward the street where we were finally allowed to drink. They didn't have to bark those orders. The crowd happily drank every drop of water and broth.

There were makeshift outhouses nearby that became quite popular once people finished drinking. Erich, Hans, and Karl-Heinz excused themselves to stand in line while the rest of us finished our broth and water.

"I wish I had more," Helga grumbled.

"Be happy you have any at all," Mother reminded her as she helped Egon and Inge drink their fill.

"I think it tastes pretty good." Elfriede wiped her mouth with the back of her hand and ventured a smile.

"You would." Helga shook her head.

"Girls!" Mother reprimanded her two oldest daughters with a hushed voice. "Now is not the time to pick at each other. Let's all try to blend in. Don't talk. Don't bring attention to yourselves."

Helga and Elfriede nodded, understanding completely. They, too, had heard horror stories about women in conquered countries who encountered the Red Army war machine. It was enough to sober them completely.

By the time all the prisoners had been fed and allowed to relieve themselves, the sun was beginning to slide down behind the horizon and the soldiers were anxious to get us back inside. They yelled something at us all and pointed toward the double doors. Hustling, we lined up and slowly walked back in through the main doors.

Our clique had remained intact while we were outside and continued to do so inside. Once more, we were sitting next to Max, Ernst and the Meier family, except now Karl-Heinz and Hans now sat side-by-side and Helga had mysteriously moved closer to Erich. Perhaps we were all struggling for something familiar to give us some semblance of control in our situation or maybe we just found a certain unity in belonging to this small clan from the Bremen-Hannover area. Either way, a bond had formed on that very first day of captivity.

Every day became a dull occupation of passing time while hunger, thirst, and the simple act of relieving oneself proved to get the best of people. Just as Mother had feared, there were those in the crowd not to be trusted and they showed themselves rather quickly. One elderly gentleman, obviously at his wit's end for food, overheard another man plotting an escape during one of the meals. The elderly gentleman found an opportune time to relay that information to our German-speaking captor who promptly handed the would-be escapee over to subordinates. We never saw that man again, but the elderly snitch received an extra helping of broth for the next several meals. He also received a cold shoulder from those he had been seated beside.

One young lady, who apparently spoke a little Russian, managed to convince a Soviet soldier that she had learned valuable information from a person seated near her. She traded the information and that person's freedom for nothing more valuable than extra time to go the outhouse when she wanted. She may have been happy to have newfound privileges but she, too, found she was thereafter shunned by those around her.

We were fed meals of broth and water twice a day and at a night we slept on the wooden floor. Each night I rolled my coat up in a ball, forming a makeshift pillow, anything to have some level of comfort on the hard floor. But every morning I awoke feeling sore and stiff next to strangers as caked with dirt and dried mud as we were. It wasn't long before the floor itself was layered in dirt as it was brushed off our clothes and flaked off our skin. But worse, there were sick individuals all around us, coughing and sneezing. Even Egon's nose was runny. Mother felt his forehead each day and gave thanks he was not running a fever, but it was evident that in the mix of dust and filth accumulating on that floor, sickness and disease were brewing. It was a less than sanitary environment.

A week after being confined in the massive room, Hans Meier woke up scratching his head. Before long, Egon and Waltraut were also scratching relentlessly and Inge complained that her "hair tickled." Frau Meier and Mother shared a worried look, but I didn't understand the significance. My hair was just as matted and I found myself reaching up involuntarily, imitating their scratching motions.

"Muttiiiii…." Helga drawled as she looked more closely at my head.

"I know." Mother nodded and began assigning jobs to the older siblings. "I need each of you to check one of your brothers or sisters."

"Check us for what?" I asked, echoing the confused look on the faces of my younger sisters and brother.

"Lice," Mother answered quietly.

I vaguely remembered that term from school in Bremen and was mortified that it was now being applied to not only me, but most every person in my family and the Meier family. Only our mothers, Erich Meier,

Helga, and Elfriede had escaped the nuisance, but the rest of us were not so fortunate. There was no powder, no medication, nothing we had at our disposal to rid ourselves of the pesky parasites. Instead, Mother and Frau Meier instructed a non-infected family member to sit behind one of us, methodically go through our hair a few strands at a time, and simply search out the nits or the pesky little bugs. They would then pull them out and kill them, hoping a daily search and kill operation would do the trick.

If there had ever been a time in my life that I was at my worst, this was it. My clothes were filthy, my skin was dirty, I'm sure I smelled, my hair was matted, and now it was filled with lice. My brothers, sisters, and I were such a sight that I truly understood the phrase "a face only a Mother could love."

But, lice and dirt and broth were nothing compared to what we soon realized was happening every night in our locked "prison." Several of our guards were selectively taking women from the crowd at night—sometimes after most everyone was asleep, other times when there were plenty of wide-awake witnesses. And who was to protest? The Red Army could flaunt their power over us by taking who they wanted, when they wanted. At first, I didn't catch on to what was occurring, but I remember overhearing my Mother and Frau Meier whispering about those women who were taken and the fact that they never returned.

One night as I lay on the hard floor, lice-ridden hair and all, I was having trouble going to sleep in the darkened room. It seemed I had been awake for hours, tossing and turning, trying to get comfortable and stop my mind from racing. Just when I felt myself nodding off, I saw two Soviet soldiers guarding one of the locked doors across the room from us move away from their post and begin pacing the floor. I didn't dare move, but covertly watched them, praying they wouldn't make their way to our side of the room. Their conversation was muted, but it was laced with quiet, guttural laughter. It was the first time I remember hearing laughter that scared me.

The two men didn't waste much time. They stopped just a few minutes later in front of a family of four: a young woman sleeping beside her three little children. I had noticed the family several times during the past ten days. The mother had looked tired and had fretted over her three rambunctious boys, trying continuously to keep them from darting away from her grasp. Others in the crowd had helped her corral them, but worry kept her from resting and it showed in her face a little more each day. Exhausted, she slept soundly now, unaware of the attention her slight frame was garnering.

One of the soldiers tapped her leg with his booted foot, rousing her from sleep. I couldn't see the features of her face, but I heard her cautiously utter the word, *"No!"* to which the other soldier bent down and yanked her up from the hard plank floor. They laughed again as they drug her away from her sleeping children, toward the door they had been guarding moments earlier. I gasped, not wanting to believe what I was seeing. She was whimpering, "No! My children!" but she made little effort to resist the two men who outweighed her significantly. She knew it was futile. Just as they opened the locked door and exited the room, I saw her turn her head, in a last effort to see her young boys who unknowingly slept on, blissfully unaware their mother was no longer by their side.

I didn't even know the young woman, but I felt myself crying for her, for me and for us all. A sob escaped me and I turned to find my mother looking over at me. She had been awake the whole time as well and she and Frau Meier had witnessed the same heart-wrenching event.

"Try to sleep now, Edith," Mother's hushed voice soothed and I lay my head down, willing myself to push the anguished lady out of my mind and find rest.

The next morning, I awoke and immediately looked across the space. The young mother was nowhere to be seen and her three young boys were scattered, being cared for by different individuals who had been seated near the young family. Rumors were rampant. Word circulated she had been raped repeatedly by the soldiers throughout the night, her breasts cut off, her throat slit, and her dead body disposed of. It was a gruesome, horrific story to absorb, making me even more terrified of our captors than before.

Max and Ernst were also acutely aware of our captors' increasingly more aggressive actions toward defenseless women each night and they looked concerned. They knew their *own* fates, as German soldiers, could be even worse at the hands of the Soviets. The two men were, of course, outnumbered and certainly no match physically in their present condition. While Max appeared to be somewhat strengthened by the daily rations we were fed, Ernst's wounded leg was becoming more and more painful. Whenever there was an opportunity, Mother and Frau Meier were more and more absorbed in solemn, inaudible discussions with Max and Ernst, and I wondered what they could be discussing so intently with the two soldiers. I would soon find out.

Late one night, I felt someone gently shaking my shoulder. I had been sleeping soundly despite the hard floor beneath me, and in the quiet, dimly lit room, I shrugged my arm, sure I was dreaming. When I felt the shaking grow more urgent, I finally opened my eyes and realized Karl-Heinz was trying to wake me up.

One by one, we were all awakened and immediately quieted by Mother's single finger planted across her lips. Confident we were all facing her, Mother peered around at the figures of others sleeping around us before speaking. Her voice was low and calm, just above a whisper.

"Children, listen to me closely. You must be very, very quiet. No words, no noise. Do you understand?"

We all nodded solemnly.

"All right, then," she said. "Follow me."

TEN

LOST

APRIL 1945

As we slowly stood and stepped away from our "beds" in the building, I realized we weren't alone. The three members of the Meier family were also involved in this clandestine operation, and both our families were being led by the two German soldiers. I wasn't sure where we were going, but it was obvious the adults had hatched some type of plan.

And that plan seemed to be leading us out of our "prison."

Our little group meandered slowly across the wooden floor, stepping over sleeping bodies, toward the doors at one side of the space, which now stood unguarded and unlocked. I was hoping my heart wouldn't beat too loudly, sure the sound would thunder against the walls and awaken the entire crowd.

As we attempted to leave, we did our best to minimize the noise we were making. Ernst had wrapped an arm around Max's shoulder so he could carry his crutches, and Inge and Egon were riding piggy-back on Helga and Mother. Apparently Mother was determined to take the stroller, but rather than risk the wheels squeaking, Erich Meier was cradling it like a child.

Elfriede was next with Waltraut, Karl-Heinz and I followed them, and Frau Meier and her youngest son Hans brought up the rear.

I assume the German soldiers had been watching the Soviets each night, noticing them gradually becoming more lax in guarding the doors while their captives slept. Over the two-week period we had been there, the guards had slipped into a nightly pattern. They either left their post to molest some woman or drink away the boredom of their time on duty. I had also witnessed that same guard-free doorway late at night, but I had no idea what would be *outside* that same door once we left the building. I felt a chilling dread, but I tried to push it out of my mind as I continued to follow my family and our little party of escapees toward that unguarded exit.

Max slowly pushed on the door. The hinges creaked and I closed my eyes, praying the noise would stop. It did. Max paused in the open doorway, peering cautiously outside, to one side and the other, before motioning us to follow. If anyone in the room woke up and followed our lead, I never knew. Once I left that building, I never looked back. I was too terrified to do so.

We had exited behind the structure. The sky was overcast with little light to guide us, but as we stumbled to a war-torn building nearby, we were able to blend in against what was left of its stone facade. Max had us stay there, unmoving, while he scouted the area. I knew the consequences if the Soviets found we had escaped, so I sat frozen against the crumbling stone wall of the burned-out building.

There was no one within sight, no movements near us, but I could hear the faint murmur of voices echoing off walls making it difficult to determine the location of those individuals who were speaking. I heard Karl-Heinz swallow and knew he was as afraid as I was.

After what seemed hours, Max returned, reporting on what he'd found to Ernst, Mother, and Frau Meier, while the rest of us listened intently. "There's a small number of military personnel eating and drinking in front of the building, but the others are down the street in the city center and I saw very little movement there. I think most of those men are sleeping."

"We've got to keep moving tonight." Ernst rested an arm on one crutch. "We have the cover of night and they'll never be more disengaged."

"Or drunk," Max interjected hopefully. The two soldiers discussed a plan of action to get out of town and into the forested countryside as quickly as possible. Moving southward seemed the best route to avoid the path of the Red Army surrounding the town and doing so kept us from traveling the main roads. It was also the closest trajectory to woods giving us more seclusion as we walked. It was a hasty plan based solely on what little Max had seen, but once Max and Ernst were both happy with their strategy, they turned to Mother and Frau Meier.

"Ladies." Max looked over at the two women. "I know we discussed this earlier, but I want to remind you both—you realize going with us risks your lives and your children's lives if we are caught."

Frau Meier swallowed and looked over at Mother for her reaction. Mother never hesitated.

"Gentlemen, when you first spoke of escaping, you agreed to let us follow you—we knew the risk then and we understand it now. I fear *more* what would happen to my children if we remained captives of the Red Army."

"But aren't you concerned we will all slow you down?" Frau Meier fretted.

Ernst lifted his injured leg and let out a muffled laugh. "*I* may slow *you* down. Look, you've already helped me by tending to this wounded leg for the past two weeks. Maybe I can return the favor by helping you both get your families back home. And if *we* travel with *you*, we'll blend in more. Our uniforms certainly make us stand out."

"Besides," Max added more seriously, "Hannover is on the way to Bremen. We'll have to part ways at some point, but we'll be able to stay with you for most of the journey."

Mother nodded her approval, as did Frau Meier, and we walked in the opposite direction of the city center, careful to watch our steps and make as little noise as necessary while making as much progress as possible. Max took the lead, with the rest of us in pairs behind him and Erich Meier—still carrying the stroller—and Ernst completing our small group. We walked for several blocks before the distance between structures began stretching out, alerting us to the fact we were on the edge of town. At one point we heard planes flying overhead, but Max encouraged us to continue walking, confident we were too far below to be spotted by pilots and were well camouflaged against the dark ground.

Once we reached the outskirts of town, we were able to pick up our pace and were soon scampering across a dirt road and a small meadow. Reaching the edge of the woods, we continued to run until we were well hidden under the canopy of the tall trees.

"Let's rest here for a while," Ernst said, hobbling on his crutches to a tree where he leaned against the bark. Max nodded and we all dropped to the ground, thankful for a breather.

"Will the soldiers come looking for us?" Karl-Heinz asked Max, worry evident in his voice.

"No one is following us, so it doesn't appear they saw us leave tonight. They probably won't miss us until morning," Max reassured my brother, "which means we need to put some miles between us and them before then. Are you up to it?"

Karl-Heinz nodded and Max looked around at all of us as we caught our breath. He directed his next comments to Frau Meier and Mother.

"Only a few minutes more and then we must be off again. Even when they realize we're gone, I don't think our captors would waste much time pursuing us. Why search for thirteen escaped prisoners and risk losing so many more by leaving the room unguarded? Still, by the time the sun comes up, I'll feel better if we are far away from town."

After about ten minutes or so, Mother walked around to each of us to ask if we felt rested enough to begin walking once more. When she reached Erich Meier she smiled.

"We could have left this stroller behind, but I know it will come in handy during the long trip back to Bremen. Now that we are going to start walking, I'm going to let Egon be pushed in it again, but I want you to know you have done something very nice for my children and for me. You carried that stroller so it wouldn't make noise in the building and then you ran all this way with it until we needed to use it again. You are good young man, Erich. *Danke.* "

Helga obviously agreed with Mother, which explained the silly looking grin on the teenager's face as she looked up at him admiringly. If Erich didn't know Helga was infatuated with him, he must have been blind! Since first meeting him, she had flirted, batted her eyes, and had mutated into a "bashful" young lady. I sighed. I hoped I never felt that way about a boy. It was ridiculous.

Swiping away the dirt from our clothes, we all stood and began trudging around the trees in front of us, staying in the protective confines of the woods. The farther we walked into its depths, the thicker and wider the forest became. It felt safe and secluded, and though it would certainly be free from Russian patrol trucks, there was still the possibility we might encounter infantry. I tried not to think about the "what ifs" and simply kept moving forward.

Sometime before the sun's rays began to lighten the eastern sky, we stopped again, feeling more confident we had escaped recapture by the Red Army. Ernst, in particular, looked exhausted and I'm sure his arms were sore from using his crutches across the uneven landscape. Hans and Karl-Heinz found a small creek and we each slurped a few handfuls of water before landing on the hard ground on the forest's edge for some much needed sleep.

When I next opened my eyes, the morning sky was a light blue hue with an occasional wispy cloud leisurely floating by. The creek water splashed lightly against pebbles on its way downstream and I could hear the even breathing of those around me. I lay quietly, looking around at the unscarred landscape around us. I could almost imagine I was in another land and time that hadn't been part of this long, drawn out war. If it was true that the war was ending, I could only feel a sense of relief. At nine, living through war had been trying and tedious, but it was also all I knew. I longed for a normal life where I could run and play and sleep without worry. What a luxury!

Turning my head, I realized some of our party was missing. I rested my hands against the hard earth and raised my upper body to look around more closely. Max was gone, as was Erich Meier and Helga. Alarmed, I was about to wake Mother and tell her when I heard footsteps approaching. Without hesitation, I dropped back to the ground and turned my head in the direction of the noise. Within minutes, I saw Max walking toward us, a smiling Erich and Helga tagging along behind him.

By this time, Ernst, Mother, and Frau Meier had awakened at the sound of the advancing trio. Hans, Karl-Heinz, and Elfriede sat up as well. After Max and company walked into our little makeshift camp, the three fell to their knees and only then did I realize they had each been carrying something. They dumped their load on the ground near us.

"Breakfast is served." Helga laughed.

A mix of carrots and cabbage rolled to a stop at our feet and Mother smiled. "My, you three have been busy this morning! I'm sure you didn't find a market nearby, so just where did you find all of this?"

"From an obliging farmer," Erich volunteered, looking at Helga and sharing a secret smile.

"Well," Max drawled, "I'm not sure about the 'obliging' part, but his garden was at least cooperative."

Mother shook Inge, Waltraut, and Egon from their sleep as the raw vegetables were passed around. "I've always taught my children it was wrong to take something that wasn't theirs, so I only hope the poor farmers in the German countryside will forgive us."

Frau Meier accepted some cabbage from Helga and nodded. "Marta, I think they would do the same under these circumstances to see that their children were fed."

Mother broke carrots in more manageable pieces for the younger ones while Erich took some food to Ernst so he wouldn't have to move. He nodded his gratitude and took a bite from a carrot. My stomach chose that moment to growl and everyone laughed.

"Edith," Karl-Heinz kidded me, "you'd better start in on that cabbage— it sounds like you really need it."

I laughed, too, and bit into what I was sure was the best tasting cabbage I'd ever eaten in my entire nine years on Earth. I chewed slowly, savoring that cabbage with every bite. I knew it might be a long time between meals, so I wanted to make every morsel count. Elfriede handed me half a carrot and I cherished every bit of it as well. Though there wasn't enough food to make us full, it was enough to satisfy our hunger for the moment and we hoped it would give us enough fuel for the next leg of our journey.

"All right everyone," Mother called out to us, "we must be going shortly, so drink some water from the creek and then find a private place in the woods to relieve yourself."

After several more minutes we reassembled on the forest's edge and were ready to start our day's journey. It was obvious Helga had every intention of staying close by Erich's side and though Mother liked the boy, she was also careful to make sure there was only so much togetherness between him and her eldest daughter. She very deliberately assigned Helga the first turn at pushing Inge in the stroller.

"But, Mutti—" Helga began as Mother took Egon's hand.

Mother had already begun walking, but turned her head slightly to look in her daughter's direction. "Yes, Helga?"

Recognizing the steely resolve in Mother's voice, Helga reluctantly took hold of the stroller and began pushing. "Oh, never mind."

Her disappointment was short-lived, however. Erich dropped into step beside her and the two teens were soon chatting away as if they were on a Sunday stroll.

Max again took the lead and Mother was relieved that burden had been removed from her shoulders. Instead, we all followed closely behind as Max set a pace that was both tiring, but manageable for the women, children, and crippled friend he led. We stayed in the shadows of the forests as much as possible during the day, but also walked the less-traveled dirt roads of the rural countryside from time to time as well. But wherever we walked, we were on the watch for Russian patrols, knowing they would use any means possible to keep us in east Germany.

We zigzagged for hours, through farmland and small communities, staying away from populated areas. We found a few nuts and berries, but nothing more substantial to munch on. Instead, we did our best to cover as much ground as possible, knowing when we stopped for the night we would take the time then to find more food. By late afternoon, tired, but driven by fear, we felt fortunate we had not seen any Soviets patrolling the countryside and were determined to keep our minds occupied so we wouldn't dwell on that fear. Karl-Heinz and Hans in particular had become fast friends in the short time they had known each other and walked side-by-side deep in conversation.

"Mutti," Karl-Heinz called ahead to where Mother walked, "what date do you think it is? Hans thinks it is the first of May, but I think he's wrong."

Mother glanced around at the budding trees, the hints of green that were beginning to make themselves known against the burnt, battle-scarred ground. It was a valid question and one Mother had not stopped to think about lately. We had no idea of an accurate time and we had lost all track of the calendar.

"Well," Mother mused. "I know we left Krumhermsdorf at the end of March and walked for about two weeks before being detained. And I believe we were held by the Soviets for about two weeks before we escaped, don't you think?"

Frau Meier, who was behind Karl-Heinz and Hans, agreed. "Yes, I believe you're right."

"So, that would mean, it's probably about the end of April," Mother said, helping Egon over the stump of a tree. "Oh, Karl-Heinz, that means you have officially turned twelve years old!"

"Happy birthday!" I laughed.

"Yes, happy birthday!" Each sibling's wish tumbled over the next, calling out their congratulations.

"When is your birthday, Karl-Heinz?" Frau Meier asked as we walked on.

"April twentieth!" Karl-Heinz smiled, exulting in the attention.

"So, he shares a birthday with the Fürher." Hans elbowed the birthday boy.

Mother shook her head in disgust. "Yes, but I doubt Hitler will have the same lavish celebrations *this* year that he usually has. By the way, son, I suppose your gift is knowing that you will be home soon."

Karl-Heinz looked at Mother with sincerity. "That is enough."

"How long will it take us to get home, Mutti?" Elfriede asked as she brushed an outstretched limb from her path.

"I don't know. Max says he's heard the British and Americans have set up border crossings between east and west, so that's our first objective—getting to that border and showing our identification proving we belong in the west. I just hope the Soviets don't prevent us from getting there."

"Where do you think we are, Mutti?" I asked.

"I'm not sure, Edith. I know we're southwest of Dresden, but I don't know where exactly." Mother looked back at me as she moved forward over brush and broken twigs.

Egon tugged on Mother's hand and looked up at her with big, soulful eyes. "Are we lost?"

Mother laughed reassuringly. "No, Egon, we're not lost. We're just… going to walk in the right direction until we see home."

Though Egon seem completely satisfied with that answer, Helga would have been perfectly happy being lost in the woods with Erich. Poor Inge could have jumped out of the stroller at any point and Helga would never have noticed. She was so engrossed in her blonde-headed escort walking by her side, I'm not sure she was aware of much around her. Frankly, though, Erich seemed just as smitten. The boy stood several inches taller than Helga, with an easy smile and pleasant personality, and he had seen as little of the surroundings as had Helga. By now, I was sure they had talked enough to know everything there was to know about one another.

We had just topped a hill after angling through another endless field crisscrossed by fences. The sun was dropping low in the sky, early evening shadows beginning to trick the eye when suddenly Ernst's strained voice carried from the back of our small caravan to the front. "Max! I see trucks coming!"

Max's head snapped around, scanning a nearby dirt road, hoping Ernst was mistaken. Though he couldn't hear the engines, he saw what Ernst had seen: a pair of headlights piercing the dusky light in the distance. It wasn't too close at the moment, but within a matter of minutes the truck would only be feet from us.

"Over there, Max!" Ernst pointed in the opposite direction from the road. Barely visible in the fading light, we could just make out a wooded area beyond a field sloping downward, out of sight of the road.

"Röpkes! Meiers! To those woods. Let's go!" As we ran, Max herded us from behind, crooking his arm, motioning for us to move immediately down the field toward the grove of trees.

We were running as fast as we could. Mother wrapped her right arm around Egon, who was perched on her hip, while she held Waltraut's hand tightly with her other hand. Erich and Helga held the sides of the stroller between them with Inge bouncing madly in the seat, Karl-Heinz ran beside Hans who had grabbed his mother's hand, and Elfriede and I were making a mad dash behind Ernst who was moving his crutches with lightning speed.

As if we needed any more encouragement to hurry, Max confirmed our worst fears. "It's a Russian patrol!"

I'm not sure what time American Jesse Owens had run in the 1936 Berlin Olympics, but my lungs screamed that I must be going much faster. My legs could not possibly pump with more speed, but just before we reached the tree line, Karl-Heinz, who had broken off into the lead, came to a screeching halt. "Stop! There's a barbed wire fence!"

The setting sun had hidden the slender lines of wire from our sight. A few minutes more and we might all have been severely injured. Instead, we came to a sudden halt in front of the fence, temporarily immobile with indecision.

Ernst threw both his crutches over the top of the fence and leaned his injured leg against the nearest fencepost for support. Holding up the bottom wire, he ordered me and Elfriede to hit the ground. "Under, crawl under… *now!*"

Blindly obeying, I scooted on my stomach through the dirt under the barbed wire and stood on the other side, watching Elfriede and Karl-Heinz quickly following my lead. Erich had the presence of mind to pull Inge from the stroller and hand her to Helga before tossing the stroller over the fence to land near Ernst's crutches. Grabbing another lower strand of wire between the next set of posts, Erich told Mother to start another line. By the time the truck was closest to us, we had all shimmied under the barbed wire and were lying flat against the sloped ground. As the truck turned on the road above, the headlights scanned an arc above our heads and continued shining away from us as they drove on.

Egon had been scratched and was crying quietly, the hem of Frau Meier's dress was ripped, and a wheel had broken off the stroller after it was tossed over the fence, but we had eluded capture and were thankful we would only have a few bruises and sore muscles after our narrow escape. We waited a few minutes and made our way to the trees. Too shaken to look for food and not really hungry after our ordeal, we went to sleep and hoped the next day would begin better than this day had ended.

The next day Karl-Heinz and Hans found some fruit that they passed around for all of us to share before we began our daily trek westward. Slowly throughout the next few hours, our path drifted toward a well-traveled roadway. We had gone from inconspicuously walking through rural farmland with our band of thirteen individuals, to being pushed along almost involuntarily in a swelling mass of evacuees that numbered into the hundreds. The crowd was confining and claustrophobic, and before long the flow of foot traffic led us toward a heavily damaged town.

We were jostled around and Mother reminded us all to stay close to each other as the crowds became more encroaching. Elfriede was now in charge of pushing Egon in the stroller—which now had only three wheels—while Mother held onto Inge, and Helga held Waltraut's hand. Ernst's leg was throbbing after the exertion the night before, so Erich left Helga's side to check on the injured soldier and provide what assistance he could.

By midafternoon we had reached the bombed storefronts in the town and Max dropped back, falling into step beside Mother and Frau Meier. "I'm hearing that the Americans have a set up a border crossing into western Germany on the edge of the next city."

"Then we need to stay on this road with these crowds?" Mother asked with some concern.

"Yes." Max nodded, wiping grime from his forehead with the back of his hand. "But, the Red Army will be actively preventing people from crossing the border from east to west. I think we continue walking a little longer today until we're out of this town and near the next city, then find a place to rest for the night. We'll rise early when fewer people will be traveling and then try to get to the border without being stopped."

The two women agreed and just as Mother turned to relay the message to Helga, an elderly man in the crowd stumbled on the mortar-damaged street into Karl-Heinz and the two fell to the cobblestoned pavement. Those nearest the commotion stepped out of the flow of human traffic to help the old man to a sitting position while Hans and Helga helped Karl-Heinz to his feet.

Our entourage stopped and clustered together on the edge of the street while Mother made sure Karl-Heinz had not been injured, allowing the masses to continue on through the town without us.

"You've hit your head, Karl-Heinz," Mother said as she touched a bump that had formed on his temple. "And your pants are torn—your knee is bleeding."

Karl-Heinz brushed her hand away, not wanting to worry her. "Yes, but I'm fine. It doesn't hurt and my knee is just scraped."

Mother wasn't convinced, but after a few moments of checking him over, she relented.

Max stood to one side of our circle and eyed Ernst closely as well. "And how is your leg holding out, Ernst?"

The soldier grunted. "I've been better, but I'll be fine. At least both of my crutches work, which is more than I can say for that rickety stroller."

Elfriede wiped sweat from her brow. "It *is* a job balancing this thing now."

Frau Meier had been taking in the dirty faces within our circle and suddenly gasped. "Where's Erich?"

Helga spun around to take in each face. Erich was nowhere to be found.

"He was standing beside me just moments ago," Ernst echoed the confusion seeping through our conversation.

"Erich! *Erich!*" Frau Meier yelled frantically as she ran toward the throngs passing by. She ran back to us with a look of sheer terror. "I must find him! Where can he be among all these people?"

"Wait!" Max reasoned. "Let's not go running off in different directions or we'll all be separated."

Max made all the children sit down near a bombed-out storefront and put Ernst in charge of overseeing. Even though we weren't to move, we had our orders. Max demanded that each of us scan the passing faces in case Erich was among them. In the meantime, he ordered Mother to take Karl-Heinz while he went with Frau Meier and Hans in search of the missing teenager. The plan was for his team to search the crowd in one direction while Mother's team searched the crowd in the opposite direction. Both teams would meet back up at the damaged storefront.

Helga was as distressed as Frau Meier was as we sat waiting on the outcome of their search. My heart pounded with fear. Somehow Erich had been separated from us in the crowd, but where could he be? Ernst did his best to console Helga, assuring her they would find Erich shortly, but I could tell Ernst was worried. Even Elfriede did her best to distract Helga by talking non-stop about anything and everything.

A couple of hours or so passed, and neither set of searchers had returned. We all grew quiet with worry. We watched for Erich as the lines of people walked passed the storefront where we sat. We called his name when we thought we recognized him, but all for naught. Judging by the sun setting on the horizon, three or four more hours had elapsed before we finally saw Mother and Karl-Heinz walking toward us. They had not found Erich. Mother sat down beside us, visibly shaken, no doubt pondering how she would feel if one of her children was missing. After another thirty more minutes, it was getting dark. Finally, we saw Max, Frau Meier, and Hans approaching from the other direction. Helga gasped and we all stood eagerly, hoping to see Erich by their sides.

He was not.

ELEVEN
THE PUSH FOR THE BORDER
APRIL 1945

As night fell, we all struggled emotionally; Frau Meier and Hans were inconsolable. Our plans for getting to the border crossing were put on hold. Max and Ernst assured us all that we wouldn't move on until we had found Erich. While that resolve and unity seemed to give Frau Meier hope, it did nothing to lessen her tears. She was a broken woman. Her husband, a pilot in the Luftwaffe, hadn't written her since leaving for a major offensive in the Ardennes Forest months before, and now her firstborn son was missing as well. It was, as she sobbed to our mother through the night, almost too much to endure.

Helga, too, was extremely upset. It had been no secret that she and the teenage boy had been interested in each other, so we were not surprised she was grieving along with his mother and brother. I felt sad—and guilty. In the weeks before, I had seen Helga's budding admiration for Erich as nothing more than another youthful infatuation on her part, and had doubted her sincerity. Based on the ridiculous way she acted when she was around him, I had doubted her sanity as well. But, now I was witnessing how genuine caring could be turned so quickly to a crippling heartbreak. My own heart ached alongside hers.

Though still in the throes of sorrow, we had to take care of the business at hand and that meant finding shelter. There were plenty of wrecked shells of buildings in town where we could bed down for the foreseeable future, so Max found one in particular that seemed well suited for our group— what had one time been a small restaurant. The walls still stood, but the ceiling had two entire expanses blown out exposing the night sky. Broken stone and glass littered the floor, but we all worked together to clear spaces for sleeping by moving larger stones and gingerly tossing out most of the windows' remnants. For the first time in more than a week, we had a roof, or least a partial roof, over our heads, but no one felt like celebrating.

It rained that first night, further dampening our mood. We had no food either, but I don't remember anyone being very hungry anyway. Poking around the room, Karl-Heinz rummaged through a dislodged cabinet which had survived the bombing and found some bowls that were still intact. Ernst and Max strategically placed the bowls around the room to catch the rainwater, so by morning we each had water to drink. Max and Karl-Heinz rose early to search the town for something to eat and they were able to find pears for each of us. No one asked where they had found them—we didn't really care.

And so the day began. Helga or Elfriede would take turns watching the younger children inside the restaurant, the older children would sit or stand outside to scan the passing refugees, and the adults would team up and walk in different directions scouring the roads for any sign of Erich. The hundreds of faces going by each hour became blurs, and Erich's name became a call that was so often repeated and so often ignored that we eventually abandoned voicing it at all.

At sundown, the adults returned. No one asked the question on the tip of our tongues—we knew the answer. It was written all over Frau Meier's face. Her eyes were red-rimmed and swollen, she had not slept at all the night before, and fatigue was gaining control of her body and soul. We parted and allowed her to enter the abandoned restaurant, but she didn't speak or seem to notice any of us. She was numb and in total despair.

Hans slowly walked into the building following his mother, his head bent to hide the tears flowing down his face. We stayed outside, giving them time alone, but we could hear her sobs drift out of the mangled walls and evaporate into the cool night air. Mother did her best to keep us talking so the Meiers could have some semblance of privacy, but it was hard to carry on a conversation when there was so much sadness so near where we stood.

At some point, we realized the crying had subsided and in its place we could hear Hans' voice, low and consoling. We couldn't hear what he was saying, and we didn't want to do so, but based on how quiet his mother had become, we realized that twelve-year-old Hans had just traded places with his mother. He was now the "adult" soothing the hurt, tending the wound. It was a moment frozen in time and one I knew I would always remember with clarity.

For two more days, we repeated the same schedule, and for two more days we had the same result. Each night just before we slept, Mother would lead us all in prayer for Erich's safety. And even though Frau Meier's emotions were more controlled since Hans had spoken with her, the prayer would renew her tears and Mother would inevitably join in. But Mother's empathy with her friend's plight not only provided support, it provided strength. After all, the two women from Bremen shared the same losses: their husbands were missing and now their first-born sons were missing as well. It was a common thread that bound them together.

By the third night, Max and Ernst took both women outside to speak privately.

"I don't want to sound disrespectful," Max began, "but we must make some very hard decisions."

Ernst kept his eyes down, scuffing a crutch against debris in the street before clearing his throat. "You know we have done everything possible to find your son while we've been here—"

"The fact is," Max said, "we've been talking with some of the other soldiers we've met in the last few days, and they say it's only a matter of time before the Soviets increase their patrols in this area."

"We're so close to the American border crossing, I'm surprised we haven't seen the Soviets before now." Ernst agreed.

"You're saying we must leave," Mother completed their unspoken thoughts.

"Yes," Max replied bluntly. "I don't want to upset you, Frau Meier, but we have to think of both of you and the rest of your children. And, I admit, Ernst and I are thinking selfishly as well. If we stay here much longer, it may be too late to leave; the Soviets could detain us and keep us from crossing into the west. If we wait, your families may never get back to Bremen and we may never see our own families in Hannover."

"There's every reason to believe that Erich may have continued on, crossed the border somehow and is now in the west," Ernst interjected. "You would not be abandoning your search. You would just be postponing it until you are safely back home."

All eyes turned to Frau Meier. She couldn't speak for several minutes, but a single tear trickled down her cheek.

Mother took her friend's hand in her own and looked at her squarely in the eyes. "I know your heart. I understand completely. But they are correct. Right now, you must take care of yourself and you must take care of Hans. Once we are back in Bremen, I promise you I will do everything in my power to help you find Erich."

The tired, slender woman seemed to have aged in the last few days and it showed in her eyes as she raised her head. She wiped her face dry, then laid her other hand over Mother's, sandwiching Mother's hand between her own, and shook her head. "No. When we are back in Bremen, we will both work *together* to find Erich… and *we* will work to find Günter and our husbands."

Mother nodded, placing her left palm atop their joined hands in a pact. Then turning to face the two German soldiers, Mother asked, "Gentlemen, when do we make the push for the border?"

"I think our original plan is still the best." Max faced Ernst for his assent. "Tomorrow we walk to the next city, rest for a few hours, and then leave early the next morning for the border while most of these crowds are sleeping."

"I agree." Ernst shifted his wounded leg to a more comfortable position. "Our chances of making it to the border undetected are better before the sun comes up."

With that, the adults re-entered the restaurant and explained to us why we were leaving without continuing our search for Erich. Helga took it particularly hard, but Mother and Ernst sat with her for some time and recounted the reasons it was necessary to move on. As we lay down for the night, Elfriede walked across the room and sat down beside our eldest sister. She didn't say anything to Helga, but began quietly making herself comfortable for the night. Helga turned to Elfriede with a slight smile. My older sisters had just shared a meaningful moment and had done so without a word being spoken.

As the sun rose, we were caught up in the throngs of travelers flowing out of town. It was as if we were drifting along in a strong current, being driven downstream effortlessly. We didn't have to plan where we were heading, our destination seemed pre-determined by the ebb and flow of the tide of which we were part. There was a numbness in mindlessly following, as if we were floating on our backs, eyes closed, uncaring. The crafting and designing of each day's efforts felt suspended, if only for the next few hours, and we were all eager to feel that relief, that freedom.

That steady, ever-moving course broke off into several branches late in the day when thirst drove different pockets of people to search the countryside for water. Fortunately, we overheard some of the residents of the territory relaying the location of a natural spring, and a group of twenty-five to thirty of us was able to locate it and drink our fill.

Afterward, as we sat on the ground taking a breather, Frau Meier looked around and gasped, "Where is Hans?"

"Karl-Heinz is missing, too," Mother noted, trying not to be infected with Frau Meier's nervousness. "They must be together."

"They were here just a few moments ago," Helga said, trying to calm Erich's mother.

"I can't bear it." Frau Meier was desperately trying to remain calm. "I cannot lose Hans, too."

"I'm sure they couldn't have gone far," Max said with a voice that sounded more relaxed than he felt. He stood to scan the farmland around us and abruptly stopped, focusing instead on two figures that had just rounded a barn several hundred yards from where we sat. Max grinned and pointed in the direction of the barn. "It appears our two wanderers have just returned."

The two boys came trotting back, puzzled by the stern looks on the faces of their mothers.

"Karl-Heinz!" I recognized that tone in Mother's voice and cringed for my brother. "How many times have I told you that we all must stay together?"

"But—" he began.

"And you, Hans Meier!" my mother continued. "How could you just disappear like that and make your mother worry when you know what she has been through lately?"

Hans's mouth gaped open, but he struggled to find words in the face of my mother's stinging indictment. Finally, he shook his head to gain some clarity.

"I… I apologize," he said to my mother and then to his own mother with true contrition. "Karl-Heinz and I wanted to find food for us all, and I just didn't realize we had been gone long enough to worry you. I promise, I won't worry you like that again."

Frau Meier was so relieved she could do little more than close her eyes and smile, but Mother was not quite ready to let the boys off the hook so easily.

"And what do *you* have to say, Karl-Heinz?"

"Sorry," he said sheepishly, but then his face lit up with a big grin. "But, we did find something to eat, Mutti."

Karl-Heinz elbowed Hans and the two boys fell to their knees. They uncurled their shirts and several dozen brussel sprouts tumbled to the ground.

"Oooh!" five-year-old Inge exclaimed with her now all-too-familiar response to anything new and different.

That broke the tension. We all laughed heartily and began passing the tiny vegetables around so everyone had a share of our late afternoon meal. Once we had finished, Max and Ernst reminded us we needed to travel more before calling it a day.

The sun was sinking below the western horizon, painting the day's last clouds with rich hues of fuchsia and royal blue before the sea of humanity slowed to rest for the night. We were on a hill overlooking the city. The border crossing should be just beyond the city limits. From our vantage point, we could look down on the urban setting—or what was left of it. Daylight was fading, casting ghostly shadows across the landscape and the remains of what had once been a thriving metropolis. Homes were destroyed, church spires were gone, shops were shattered, replaced by jagged stone and crumbling walls. The streets were hidden beneath dirt and debris. Morning would reveal the full extent of the damage, but it appeared the life of the city had been extinguished. And, adding further symbolism to that death, the city was no longer able to cast a yellow glow against the sky—its lights had been extinguished as well.

Mother reminded us to rest, so we obediently lay down on the hard ground. I was sure I had just closed my eyes when I was awakened by Elfriede whispering my name repeatedly. Rubbing my face with my hands, I rose and stretched my arms to the still-darkened sky. For just a moment, I was confused. Where was I? What time was it? The first question was finally answered in my foggy brain, but as for the time, none of us knew the answer to that. I did note the moon still reigned in the quiet, starry sky.

We fell into our familiar line-up: Max leading us all with Ernst at our rear and our two families inserted in the middle. Our intent had been to be some of the few making this last leg to the border dividing east and west; the reality was there were still dozens of like-minded refugees walking with us. Max was disappointed there were so many people still marching forward, but Mother reminded him how many thousands might be making the same journey had we waited until daylight.

Trudging down the hillside, we followed the main road into the city. In the moonlight, I could make out the damage bombs had inflicted more closely, and though I was accustomed by now to seeing the aftereffects of war, I still marveled at the blanket destruction before me. We carefully stepped around potholes in what had once been quaint cobblestone streets. Shattered glass was tossed everywhere, blown from window panes from every direction. We walked by a church, almost unrecognizable had it not been for unmistakable clues: the strewn material that lay at its door was stained glass, the once proud church bell now lay on its side on the street nearby, cracked and toneless.

If I had thought the city looked ghostly from the hillside, it was nothing to walking through the near-abandoned city now. It felt like a ghost town. All I heard in the still city was the shuffling of our feet through its debris. Perhaps there were still residents resting nearby, getting ready for the work of rebuilding tomorrow, but I wondered how many people had simply fled to start a new life elsewhere or left to search for loved ones lost during the war.

Helga was back on stroller duty and was doing her best to maneuver the three-wheeled buggy around holes and craters, though it made for a bumpy ride for Egon. She had been unusually reflective since Erich's disappearance. With the exception of Günter, who was experiencing the war in ways we might never know, Helga was the one sibling who had been touched more personally than any other in our family. Being threatened by Colonel Pfiffer and now losing Erich had broken her spirit in ways that would be long-lasting. I wondered if I would even like this new Helga. Despite the fights she liked to pick and the pointed remarks she tossed my way from time to time, I enjoyed her spark of life and was sure she made me re-think so many issues. She had always kept my senses fine-tuned.

My meandering thoughts meant I was less focused on where I was walking and before I realized it, I had stepped into a pothole, stumbling forward into Helga.

"Edith!" She turned to me, wide-eyed and incredulous. She kept her voice low, but I felt the sting of her words. "Quit bumbling down the road and watch where you're going!"

All my previous sympathetic thoughts about Helga evaporated. She might be scarred emotionally, but I needn't worry about my sister—some things about her would never change. I would never admit it, but I was almost glad to know the old Helga was still around.

It felt like it took an eternity to pass through the city, but we finally found ourselves on its outskirts negotiating a long straight stretch of road. The sun was still not up, but the sky was slowly shedding its monotone backdrop for the pastels of dawn. The landscape was still camouflaged in shadows, but the early morning hues helped unmask our surroundings. And as we walked, it gradually dawned on me that the road ahead was narrowing, littered with large objects as yet not quite in focus. As we got closer, I could see the dozens of people in front of us were compressing into pairs on the left side of the road to negotiate the clutter. Slowly, the obstructions came into better view.

"Panzers!" Karl-Heinz turned to me with amazement.

Two large German Panzer tanks had been abandoned in disarray in the road. The turret of one was bent and turned at an awkward angle, the tread of the other lay broken in a line on the ground, and I could tell even in the dim light that both tanks were black from fire. I had seen tanks during a parade in Bremen years before, but I had never been this close to them before. As we walked past the metal beasts, I was stunned at their size. Each was almost 23 feet long and 8 feet high. The crippled behemoths were frightening even though they now lay silent and impotent.

The hatch was open on one of the tank's cupolas, but I looked away, afraid I might see a lifeless body half-escaped from the steel coffin. I looked instead at the feet in front of me as they marked the way around this final battleground in the middle of our escape route. Armored vehicles were also heaped together, tossed as easily as toothpicks, some in mangled piles on the road, others nose-first in ditches. I realized I had not felt heat as we had passed the tanks and vehicles, so the battle must not have happened in the last few days. I breathed a little easier. Surely the dead had been moved, so I wouldn't see bodies. But, either way, I shivered, knowing I was walking through the final hours of life for many men.

By now the sun was peeking above the horizon, banishing the blacks and grays of night for good in favor of day's vivid colors. The landscape was more in focus now and we could clearly see the long stretch of road leading up to an incline. Once we reached its peak, we stopped and observed the road ahead curving slightly and then extending again to a line of trees.

"That's it!" Max pointed.

I stepped up on tiptoe and squinted to understand what Max was seeing. At the end of the next stretch of road, a small wooden shed had been erected with a few open-topped vehicles surrounding it. I could make out groups of men standing around the area and something was barricading the road.

"The border," Mother whispered with an almost reverent tone.

"I never thought I would welcome the sight of an American," Ernst half-laughed.

Max agreed solemnly. He silently hoped the Americans would not give him and Ernst any trouble entering into the west since he was sure they would suffer more under Soviet control in the east.

About a dozen or so people were already on the long approach to the crossing ahead of us as we began the sloped descent. Ernst was behind our entourage encouraging Elfriede and Waltraut forward as two dozen other people straggled even farther back. We hadn't been on the descent more than five minutes when I heard a commotion from the group following us. Ernst was still moving ahead, but had turned his head to one side in an attempt to hear what was being said. A few minutes later he knew the issue and called ahead to Max to inform him.

"Max, I hear an engine," Ernst yelled. "Some of the people behind us think it might be a Soviet patrol."

"No time to find out if they're right," Max yelled back. He glanced at my Mother, silently signaling his concern. "Ladies, we need to pick up our speed."

Mother and Frau Meier motioned for us to walk a little faster and as we reached the final stretch to the border, we were making better time. I was beside Karl-Heinz and Hans and the three of us were stretching our legs considerably to keep up the pace the adults were setting. With the sound of the engine growing louder, Hans turned in time to see a small military truck top the incline and screech to a stop. He yelled.

"Max!"

Max had already heard the brakes of the vehicle and turned to see the same sight. Now trotting toward the border, Max kept an eye on the vehicle and watched the Soviet driver shift gears and start down the road toward us all. Three other Red Army soldiers stood in back of the truck, holding on, watching the string of refugees streaming toward the American sector.

"Hey, kids," Max called as calmly as possible. "How about we race to the border?"

With the exception of Egon, Inge, and Waltraut, I'm not really sure the rest of us were fooled by that attempt at normalcy, but it had the desired effect. We all ran toward the border, making the little wooden shed and the American soldiers our finish line. Though my lungs felt like bursting and my measured gasps for air echoed in my ears, I could still make out the sound of the approaching Soviet patrol. I wanted to cry, but fear drove me on and with Hans and Karl-Heinz running beside me, I had every incentive necessary to continue the sprint. This was not a race up the steps to the school. Falling down had more dire repercussions.

I could see two pairs of posts standing waist-high on either side of the road minutes ahead of us as the Soviets came closer and closer. A log had been cut and each end was resting on each set of posts, making a makeshift horizontal crossing "arm" across the road. The group in front of us had already been allowed to cross the border and the Americans had just physically placed the log back on the posts barring passage. We would have to stop, but for now we were running as quickly as possible toward the Americans while Ernst half-hopped, half-ran on his wounded leg.

As we got closer, three American soldiers stepped up on the other side of the log and one of them shouted, *"Halt!"*

We reached the crossing and skidded to a stop in front of them with the Soviets bearing down on us.

"I need to see identification," the same American spoke to us while another soldier repeated the instructions in German. "You cannot cross into the western sections of Germany unless you can prove you are residents there."

The Soviet truck braked several yards behind us, its engine idling. We were in no-man's land and our future lives were, very literally, about to be decided. American soldiers had stopped us from going forward and Soviets soldiers waited to take us back.

TWELVE
GERMAN ENGINEERING
LATE APRIL, EARLY MAY 1945

With the eyes of soldiers from two countries on her, Mother's hands began to shake, but she determinedly handed Inge off to me and immediately unbuttoned her dirt-grimed suit jacket. As we all watched, she shrugged out of it and threw it to the ground. Bending over, she ripped open a small section of the lining about the width of her palm. Reaching in with her hand, she rummaged around for a few seconds and then pulled out papers which she laid on the ground. Thumbing through the documents, she counted them and then reached in for one more. Satisfied, she grasped all the documents in her right hand, stood and thrust them toward the American GI still standing on the other side of the log.

"The documents for me and my children. We are from Bremen."

One of the American soldiers took the papers from her and shuffled through them, eyeing each one of us and alternately looking at one document at a time. I glanced around. The Soviets sat patiently in their truck, watching the process unfold as the final group of people who had lagged behind us finally reached the border and took their place in line behind us. Of the three Soviets who had stood during their ride to the border, one had jumped out and now sat in the front passenger seat, propping a boot on the truck's dash. The other two soldiers were still in the back, but now leaned over, resting their arms on the rails of the truck bed taking in the entertainment. It seemed the Red Army was content to sit by and catch the "fish" thrown back to them rather than make a scene in front of the Americans. I just hoped all our identification was in order.

After several excruciating minutes, the American looked up and handed the papers back to Mother. His words were translated by another soldier.

"You and your children can pass through."

Another American in uniform went to one end of the log/crossing arm and lifted it up, angling it in toward the west allowing just enough room for Mother and the rest of our family to cross into the American sector. When Helga finally pushed Egon through in the stroller, the soldier moved the end of the log back on its base, and the entire process began again with the Meiers and the German soldiers.

I knew we still had a long way to go before we were back home, but making it out of eastern Germany was a major step in that process. We breathed a sigh of relief and now only hoped that the rest of our group was allowed to cross. As it turned out, Max and Ernst were ushered across the border much faster and easier than the rest of us, but Frau Meier struggled. At some point she had entrusted Hans with their IDs and when he took them from an inside pocket of his coat, she began weeping when she saw Erich's ID with theirs. It was a reminder that her eldest son was missing and, had he somehow crossed the border before us, he would not have been able to do so without deception.

Mother stepped in and explained to the bewildered American translator why Frau Meier was so distraught. Acknowledging that the documents for the Meiers appeared to be in order, the American handed the documents back to Hans and waved them through, no doubt glad to be rid of another emotional traveler.

As we walked deeper into the American sector, I glanced back to see two families who had been behind us. They were arguing with the Americans. They had no papers confirming they were from western Germany and no amount of persuasion was going to get them across the border. The Americans were standing firm with the bare tree trunk resting between them and the refugees. I heard the translator holler, *"Next!"* and with that the two families were summarily dismissed. Looking bewildered and fearful, they stood to one side wringing hands, shouting, and continuing to make their case, but it was falling on deaf ears. Of course, not everyone was ignoring their pleas. The Soviets had gotten out of the truck and were purposefully strolling over to the refugees. I turned around and found Mother looking at me.

"Don't look back, Edith," Mother said. "Don't worry about what might have been. Just remember, we're one step closer to home."

I nodded.

"Max," Mother confided to him as she looked back at Ernst struggling to keep up on his crutches. "I'm worried about Ernst. He looks extremely fatigued and the last time I checked on his leg, the wound looked infected. I doubt we can find any medicine, but the man needs to rest. All this walking is only aggravating his injury."

Max covertly peeked back at his friend, taking in the dark circles under his eyes and the effort he has making just to keep pace. "Now that we're out of the Soviets' hands, maybe we can take a little more time to rest today than we have been doing."

"Let's try to find some shelter from the sun. I'll clean his wound as best as I can and maybe he can sleep," Mother said.

Max nodded. "Agreed. Let's keep an eye out for some suitable shelter."

We had just rounded a bend in the road when train rails came into sight beside us. "Look at the railroad tracks, Max," Karl-Heinz pointed.

An entire expanse of the railroad tracks had been bombed to disrupt rail transportation. Once straight metal rails now twisted madly in haphazard directions on the ground and in the air. In place of the rock bed that had once supported those rails was a black void surrounded by burnt grass and mounds of unearthed mud and rock. The damage stretched for another mile ahead of us and as the road mimicked the rails' path, we walked beside it, mesmerized by the sheer magnitude of the steel's contortions.

Still early morning, Max squinted to bring into focus something near the tracks some distance away. Just beyond the destruction, a small train station sat alone and forlorn in the rural countryside.

"I think we may have just found some shelter," Max confided in Mother and pointed to the wooden structure by the tracks.

By the time we reached the train station, there were already forty or fifty people who had taken shelter there, but we were able to find an empty bench and some floor space where we could all sit down. Max took Karl-Heinz and Hans with him to scout the surrounding area for food and water while Mother insisted Ernst sit on the bench.

Max and the boys returned several minutes later with potatoes and a battered tin bucket partially filled with water. "Not much for breakfast, but it will have to do."

"And look what we brought for you." Karl-Heinz smiled and handed Mother a handful of yellow and purple flowers.

Not to be outdone, Hans presented his mother with a small bouquet of wildflowers as well. "Max found them."

"But it was our idea to pick them for you both," Karl-Heinz chimed in.

The women smiled and accepted the flowers from their sons.

"*Danke,* Karl-Heinz." Mother held the small bouquet in her hands. "It's nice to have some color back in our world again."

As we sat huddled together on the floor and bench, Mother and Frau Meier distributed the potatoes to each of us and the bucket was passed around so we could each drink.

It had been a tense morning and looking around, I was convinced everyone felt as drained as I did. I ate my potato slowly, savoring the juiciness and knowing it would satisfy my gnawing hunger if only for a little while.

While other travelers in the room were leaving to rejoin the masses on the road, our group continued to eat in silence, each person lost in thought. Inge turned up her nose after taking a single bite from her potato, but Helga "graciously" took it off our youngest sister's hands so it wouldn't go to waste.

With a little something in our stomachs, it wasn't long before Egon, Inge, and Waltraut had nodded off completely, and Helga and Elfriede were having trouble holding their eyes open. Since it seemed evident everyone had finished "breakfast," Mother was confident the rest of the water was not going to be used for drinking, so she moved the bucket beside Ernst to clean his wound.

"I'm fine, really," Ernst insisted, but Mother could hear the pain in his voice as he extended his leg.

She gingerly rolled up his pant leg and unwrapped the dirty bandage. As she feared, his wound was now swollen, feverish with infection. She glanced up at the young man. "You really need medication, but I'll do the best I can for you."

Ernst looked grim, but shook his head in recognition. "I know you will."

She set the filthy bandage to one side. "*This* will never do."

Taking off her jacket, Mother began to unbutton the cuffs of her once-white cotton blouse and began ripping the sleeves from the cuffs up to the shoulders while still wearing it.

"What are you doing, Mutti?" I asked with fascination as she continued to tear her sleeves from her blouse.

"Well," Mother said as she ripped both unattached sleeves lengthwise. "This may not be the cleanest material, but it will do to clean his wound and will make for a much fresher bandage than Ernst had before.

Karl-Heinz, would you hand me the flowers you gave me earlier?"

Picking up the hand-picked flowers, Karl-Heinz stood beside Mother.

"I'm going to keep these lovely yellow flowers," Mother said as she separated the flowers by color. "But *these* are lavender and my mother always used the oil from these as a homemade remedy."

Karl-Heinz and I watched as Mother picked the purple blooms from their stems and rubbed them together between her flattened palms over the bucket. As she did so, the ground-up blooms sprinkled over the remaining water in the bucket. When she finished, she used her hand to mix the lavender dust and water together and let the mixture sit for a while.

"Well." Ernst managed a chuckle. "Even if it doesn't have any medicinal effect, my leg will at least *smell* good."

"Yes." Karl-Heinz grinned. "You'll smell a *lot* better than Hans and me."

After a few minutes, Mother took one of the sleeves now lying on the floor and tore it into smaller strips. She picked up one of those strips and dipped it into the lavender water, carefully dabbing the wound on Ernst's leg repeatedly until she believed it was as clean and as saturated with the lavender oil as possible. Once the remedy was applied, she took the longest strip of sleeve and wrapped it around the treated wound, tying it securely.

"We'll continue to watch this and treat it with what we can find by the roadsides," Mother told Ernst. "Now, get some rest."

Ernst obeyed and was soon asleep, even though he was doing so in a slightly reclined position on the bench. As he slept, I felt myself slipping into a peaceful state somewhere between awareness and sleep. I remember bending my elbow so my arm pillowed my head on the hard floor, and despite the discomfort, I curled up and drifted into oblivion.

I'm not sure if it was the sneezing or the crying that first woke me, but I soon realized Inge was not only awake, but she was not feeling well. I had noticed her lack of appetite at breakfast, but I hadn't really attributed it to illness. Mother assured Inge she just had a cold, but the five-year-old was also running a low grade fever. And we had all learned years ago that in a family as large as ours, once one came down with something, it was just a matter of time before it made the rounds to the rest of us. Unfortunately, Inge wasn't the only one feeling sick. Though Ernst had been able to sleep for a couple of hours, he did not look well. He, too, was running a fever, though his was probably due more to his leg injury than a cold.

Mother and Frau Meier conferred with Max, expressing worry about Inge and the cold that might become prevalent among us all. But, they also knew that Ernst must have some relief from walking. Understanding their concern, Max was not sure what options were available, but left the train station with a promise to learn what he could about any other means of travel.

An hour or so later, Max returned, explaining that we were several miles from a major road. "Now that we are in the west and don't have to worry about hiding from the Soviets, we can walk openly. That means the roads will be even more crowded than before, but that should also mean more modes of transportation. Ernst, if you can make it until we get into some traffic, I'll do what I can to find something with wheels to rest that leg of yours."

Ernst let out a little laugh. "I'll make it. I'm not going to let these two women and their kids make me look bad. If they can do it, I can do it."

Max nodded. "Let's take off in a few minutes then. We'll rest again tonight."

Since Inge didn't feel well, Elfriede placed her in the stroller and pushed her back to the road while Mother held Egon's hand. Helga kept Waltraut close beside her and Karl-Heinz and I walked alongside Frau Meier. Max led us away from the train station with Hans falling behind to help Ernst in whatever way he could. We walked for a few hours, stopping only to relieve ourselves and to drink water we found in a creek along the way. When we finally reached the major road Max mentioned, I was stunned at the sea of human traffic. There were thousands of people, some carrying a single piece of luggage, others pulling small carts with what was left of their worldly possessions, and most—like us—simply walked unfettered, with nothing but what they had on.

A few people were on horseback or used their animals to pull wagons in which they let the young or very old ride. But civilians weren't alone. Now there were many more German soldiers joining the throngs walking westward. Many were injured, most were exhausted, but all looked beaten emotionally. I looked at the faces of the men and women around me and wondered how long it would take to heal our people and our country.

From time to time we had to move to the shoulder of the road to let Allied tanks, armored vehicles, or Jeeps take the road. But, we were all so numb, so tired, we did so almost automatically, barely focusing on the foreigners who were now prevalent in our country. Our concentration was on moving forward, getting one step closer to home. All else paled in comparison.

By late afternoon, we entered a city, still without hope of finding transportation. The city looked like so many others we had walked through: damaged heavily, with years to go before it would be made whole, if ever. We had just passed a row of burnt-out houses when Max insisted we stop to rest. We were all tired, but Ernst was pale and it was obvious his leg throbbed with pain, despite his refusal to admit it. While we each began sitting on the ground, Ernst kneeled, tossed his crutches down and collapsed. Inge was listless, irritable, her nose running and her eyes reflecting how badly she felt, and now Elfriede was complaining of a sore throat.

I could tell Mother was concerned. There were no hospitals open near us, but even if there had been, they couldn't possibly care for the numbers that would knock on their doors. Hotels weren't available with soft beds to rest and recuperate; and we were doing well just to find enough food and water each day to keep up our strength for the trip. It felt like we were running a marathon with unbelievable obstacles and no end in sight. I wanted to cry, but frankly, I was too tired.

Max stood with his hands on his hips, looking at the motley crew he had volunteered to lead. We looked rough. We had all lost weight over the past few weeks, but now our health was being affected by our poor diet and hygiene. It was amazing we had covered as much ground as we had under the conditions. But we had to keep moving and we needed every last bit of fortitude available to reach home. For all the bravado he may have had in his military career, Max knew he had little at his disposal to help any of us at the moment. He bowed his head, his shoulders drooped.

And that's when we heard the sound of a motor. It was the heavy churning of a military vehicle I had heard so many times before, with the occasional long grate of metal grinding as the driver changed gears. Max's head snapped sideways and Ernst immediately sat up from where he had been resting. My first reaction was fear. I was so accustomed to listening for Red Army patrols and hiding that it was hard to have any other mindset. My siblings looked as confused and unsure as I did.

"Is it a transport truck?" Ernst looked to Max for an answer, but Max was already sprinting into the street toward the Opel Blitz truck bouncing its way toward us.

He waved his arms madly in the air and the driver screeched to a halt. From where we sat, we could see Max jog to the driver's door and engage the man in dialogue. A few minutes later, Max rejoined us and began helping Ernst to his feet.

"Ladies and gentlemen," Max announced with some satisfaction, "I'm not sure how long they will have room for us, but for now we have a ride. Now, hurry! We can't keep them waiting. Everybody up!"

Hans grabbed Ernst's crutches as Max helped his friend to his feet. Mother and Frau Meier corralled the younger children as they urged the rest of us to hurry. Helga grabbed Inge, Elfriede grabbed the stroller, and we all ran down the street to the back of the transport truck. As we rounded the Opel, I looked above the wood slats boxing in the truck bed and could see the heads of a few soldiers peering over the sides at us. The bed's metal framework extended bare into the sky, no longer supporting its canvas covering, exposing the troops it carried to the elements.

When we reached the back, a few of the soldiers reached for our hands to assist. It was crowded, but several men stood and gave us their seats on the wooden benches that lined the transport bed. Max was content to stand and Ernst was given a place to recline on the floor while the rest of us huddled together on a bench. After they lifted the stroller from Elfriede's hands and sat it on the floor of the truck bed, the battered, dusty carrier balanced temporarily despite its missing wheel. For a few seconds all the soldiers watched in silence as the stroller listed precariously. When it finally fell on one side to sit at a crazy angle, the men burst out laughing.

"You pushed the young ones in that?" one man bellowed.

"Yes." Mother laughed with them. "All the way from Saxony."

Another man slapped his leg. "What kept it together?"

Mother grinned. "German engineering."

The men smiled, but her words had changed the mood.

"German engineering," one man said somberly. "We'll need a lot of that in the coming decades to rebuild what Hitler has destroyed."

As the transport driver shifted into first gear to leave the city, another soldier shook his head and leaned back against the wood panels of the truck bed. "I guess Albert Speer can stop playing architect for Hitler's grand building projects now."

Max lifted his head, "What do you mean?"

"Haven't you heard?" He looked at us. "The war is over. Germany has surrendered unconditionally."

—

Maneuvering through the multitude of travelers as we sat in the back of that transport truck was a luxury. We were packed in like sardines, but I didn't care. Walking had been slow, tedious, and tiring. In comparison, the truck seemed to be chewing up miles in lightning speed. I couldn't even remember the last time I had traveled in anything other than a train—and that had been infrequent. The ride may have been faster than walking, but it was certainly anything but smooth. We bumped along the shell-pocked roads so often that at times I had to hold on to the wooden bench just to keep from bouncing completely off my seat. And without the canvas canopy over our heads, the wind whipped our hair and faces making for a chilly ride, particularly at night. The cool air did nothing to ease Elfriede's sore throat, Inge's cold was a little worse, and now my nose was scarlet from sneezing and wiping it on my sleeve.

In deference to their newly acquired younger audience, the soldiers who stood around us used a little more caution in sharing news of the last days of the war, but they still did so with more coarse language than I was accustomed to hearing. Nevertheless, compared to the snippets of gossip we had received, these men were a wealth of information and we soaked in every word. We had lost all track of days and months, but apparently Germany had surrendered on May 7th—just a day or two before we hitched our ride with them—even though the war in the Pacific was still raging on. The soldiers had heard that the week before, Mussolini had attempted to escape detection in Italy before being discovered and shot to death. The bodies of Mussolini, his mistress, and several others had been hung upside down in front of an Esso gas station in Milan. More shocking still was news that forty-eight hours after Mussolini's demise, Hitler and Eva Braun had committed suicide in Berlin. The man who had set all this misery into motion had died a cowardly death, leaving the rest of us to face the aftereffects of his grand schemes for power.

The muffler on the Opal Blitz was damaged and managed to intermittently coat us with sooty exhaust. Needless to say, in addition to coughing from colds, we were now choking on fumes. We drove on through the night, stopping only to get water, what food we could get, and find relief in the woods. Despite the discomforts, I was not happy when the transport driver informed us we had to start walking again the next morning. Apparently, they would be taking a different route from ours.

For the next few weeks, we were back to walking during the day and sleeping in the woods or barns or just out in open fields each night. Except for bread that Karl-Heinz and I swiped in one town, our meals consisted of vegetables we could find from gardens, and fruits, nuts or berries we happened to run across on our route. Thanks to our connection with Max and Ernst, we did manage to hitch a ride with another transport that saved us a day's journey, but otherwise we were on foot for the entire journey.

I had grown accustomed to seeing American soldiers along the way. I thought they were recognizable even from a distance. They had a certain swagger and self-assuredness in the way they carried themselves. While I didn't comprehend their language, most of the soldiers were loud and boisterous, yelling to their companions using what I assumed were very colorful epithets. They were smiling, jovial, no doubt happy the war was finally over for them in Europe, and for the first time, we even saw black American servicemen—a unique sighting for someone from Germany. But, at some point during our trek back home we passed into the British occupied zone and it was just as educational as seeing the Americans for a nine-year-old girl.

The British soldiers seemed more proper, more genteel. Maybe my view was colored from stereotypes I had heard of these foreigners, but I suppose it was fair that I romanticized them all a little. They were larger than life, they weren't stern and forbidding as the Russians had been and, though they were certainly on guard against criminal elements among the crowds, they seemed content to let us pass through to rebuild our lives so they get could back home themselves and rebuild their own lives.

We'd left Krumhermsdorf only nine weeks before, though it had seemed a lifetime ago. But we had finally reached the outskirts of Hannover, and that meant we would be parting ways—possibly forever—with Max and Ernst.

"I hear there is rail service from Hannover to Bremen," Max shared with Mother and Frau Meier. "You should be able to make the last leg of your journey by train."

Mother sighed. "That would be a blessing."

"And when you both reach Bremen, find the people with the Red Cross. They might be able to help you find news about your husbands and sons."

Frau Meier's countenance fell. She had tried her best to keep her mind off of her eldest son during the trip, but there were times the hurt was unbearable and unforgettable. She simply nodded and thanked Max for his reminder.

"Max." Mother reached out to grasp his hand. "You could have left us in that building at the mercy of the Soviets, but you didn't. We are forever grateful."

Max inclined his head toward Ernst. "You have helped Ernst tremendously, and we were going your way."

Ernst, who was looking more pale and gaunt than ever, managed a weak laugh. "I told you I would only slow you down. Your families might have been in Bremen weeks earlier if you hadn't had me hobbling along with you."

"Nonsense." Mother smiled. She patted him on the shoulder and her mood turned more serious as she added, "Ernst, please have that leg checked out as soon as possible."

"I will," he promised.

The men said their goodbyes to each of us and I felt myself getting emotional at the thought of leaving them. My father had only been in my life sporadically since he was drafted into the Army over five years before, so it had been comforting to have the two young men around.

Turning around, I watched them walk away from us. Relieved of the burden of leading our entire group, Max now only had to worry about himself and his friend. At Max's insistence, Ernst draped his arm around Max's shoulder and handed one of his crutches to him to carry, then wrapping his other arm around Ernst's waist, Max slowly began helping his wounded companion walk away. I didn't know how much farther they had to travel to make it to their homes, but I knew Ernst was almost at his limit.

I remember thinking at the time that we would keep in touch with Max and Ernst after we got back home, to see how their lives had progressed, and be assured that Ernst had gotten well. We never did. It would be the last time we would see them.

THIRTEEN
STRANGERS IN THE STREETS
MID-1945 TO 1947

We were back in Bremen and it was surreal, but after waking up on the floor of the train station, I also knew our whole ordeal was far from over. Pinning our hopes on being able to live in my grandparents' home had fallen through. My Oma's and Opa's house had been totally destroyed almost a year ago in August 1944 when my uncle Christian had lost his life during a bombing raid. We had been forced to leave all our furniture and material possessions behind in Krumhermsdorf and now that we were back home in Bremen, we were starting with absolutely nothing.

I wondered about our good friends and neighbors, the Müllers—Manfred and Uta. It had been more than a year since we had received letters from them, but seeing the desolation in the city, I now had a better sense why that might have been. No doubt, the Müller family had to seek safety outside the city and had not been able to inform us. At least, that's what I hoped had happened. The thought that they, too, may have been killed during a bombing raid in Bremen was something I didn't want to think about, I refused to think about. I would simply consider them relocated and would look forward to the day when they would return and Karl-Heinz and I would get to visit and play with our good friends again.

The Red Cross had set up feeding stations and, once again, we were standing in line for food and water. At least this time we weren't under the watchful eye of the Red Army, not to mention the food was certainly much better. After we were fed, we returned to the train station, but it was obvious we could not continue to stay there indefinitely. Bremen residents were coming back with each train that pulled into the station and it was imperative as they returned that others be moved out to some type of housing within the city.

So, that morning after we had eaten, Mother and Frau Meier left again to stand in one of numerous lines to speak with the Red Cross about finding a place to stay for our families. Late in the afternoon, the two women returned, approaching our little corner of the train station to share what they knew about our new accommodations.

"Well, children," Mother said, "we have been assigned to live above a police station for now."

"Police station?" Karl-Heinz's ears perked up. "Will be locked up in jail cells with bars and handcuffs?"

Helga looked at Karl-Heinz, shook her head, and crossed her arms. "That's ridiculous. They're just finding room for us. Although handcuffing you might be a good idea."

Mother held up her hands. "Enough arguing. The floor above the police station has several bunks and lots of room for a family our size. We should be very grateful we have a roof over our head."

"You said *our* family had been assigned there." I looked at Hans and Frau Meier. "What about the Meiers?"

Frau Meier looked over at Hans with regret. "I know you would like to stay with Karl-Heinz, Hans, but we have been assigned a smaller place across the city."

Hans and Karl-Heinz looked crushed and we all felt the same

disappointment. Our families had been through a lot together in the last two months; we were reluctant to be separated.

"Bremen is our home. We will all be staying here, so we will be seeing each other again," Mother reminded us all as she placed her hand on Frau Meier's arm. "As a matter of fact, after we are settled, we are going together to the Red Cross once more to see what they can tell us about Dirk and Günter and Erich and Herr Meier."

Frau Meier's eyes glistened as she nodded and placed her hand over Mother's hand. "Yes, I hope they will able to give us news."

"We won't stop looking," Mother assured her friend.

For the second time in as many days, we were saying goodbye to friends, but at least we knew the Meiers would be close by. Hans and Karl-Heinz shared a laugh before waving, and we left the train station with our rickety stroller in tow. As we walked, I tried to make sense of where we were, but I couldn't recognize the landscape in relation to the city I knew so well. There were simply no landmarks nearby to give me my bearings, but after walking for twenty minutes, we approached a two-story building that Mother said was our destination. The police station, like others around it, was still standing but it had no electricity and its stone structure was battered and had broken or missing windows.

Once we entered the building, Mother was given a candle and shown a flight of stairs that led to the second floor. We climbed the stairs and reached a large open room with two small windows on either end that filtered in just enough light to detail a room lined with bunk beds. Our new living quarters were totally empty otherwise—no other people were there—and we each ran to lay claim to the bed we wanted. Helga and Elfriede wanted the bunks in the far corner of the room, Mother let Waltraut and Inge have the next bunks, Karl-Heinz and I were next, and Mother and Egon took the next set of beds. There were no sheets or pillows, but each bed had fresh straw for a mattress. Though years later I would think back on that as crude, it was heavenly at the time. I had been sleeping on the hard earth so often in the weeks preceding our return to Bremen that a bed of straw was a comfortable change.

It didn't take very long for any of us to settle in that night. It was quiet. We had traveled so long with thousands of people on the road that it seemed strange to be in a room with just my family. It was also relaxing. I could stretch my legs and arms out straight and not worry about cold or bugs or rain. There was a roof over my head and I no longer had to worry about hiding from Russians. The last nights I had slept in Bremen almost two years ago were full of fear—fear of air raids, fear of running to the bunkers to escape the bombers. How different my hometown was; how different my life was. My mind was spinning with so many thoughts I could not drift off to sleep.

In a few moments, a whispered question drifted down to me. "Are you asleep, Edith?" Karl-Heinz's head suddenly appeared above me, peering down over the top bunk.

"No, I can't stop thinking," I whispered back honestly.

"Nor can I," Karl-Heinz admitted. "Wonder where Vati and Günter are? Wonder where Erich Meier is?"

Like my earlier musings on the Müllers, I wasn't sure I wanted to think about where our father and brother were. I was afraid of the answer. "Maybe Mother will find out something from the officials she will be talking to."

My brother pondered that. "Maybe. But, it may take a long time to learn anything."

"Yes, I know."

"I think Erich was captured by the Russians."

"You don't know that," I reminded my brother. "I think he just got lost. Maybe he was able to sneak across the border and will meet up with his mother and Hans back here."

"Maybe," he muttered, but I could tell he was doubtful.

There was enough light in the room that I could just make out Karl-Heinz's features. I could tell he was struggling to talk about what was really on his mind. He wrestled with it for a few more seconds and then I heard his intake of breath.

"Vati was sent to the Eastern Front, so…." Karl-Heinz hesitated. "So, he could be…."

I shook my head in the darkness. "No. No, don't say what you're thinking."

It was quiet for a minute as we both pushed the gravest thoughts away.

"Maybe Günter is still somewhere in Bremen," I countered after a while in an attempt to negate my fears about my father.

"Yes, I hope so, too," Karl-Heinz said softly. "We might be seeing him very soon."

On that more hopeful note, Karl-Heinz rolled over to face the ceiling and I smiled, optimistic that Mother might get some much-needed good news within the coming days. Thinking on my eldest brother and his propensity to impress everyone around him, I soon fell into the soundest sleep I had experienced in over two months….

…and woke to a room full of people!

Sometime during the night as I had been soundly sleeping, more families had been moved in and were now occupying almost every bunk in the entire room. So much for thoughts of isolation and solitude! We were, once more, sleeping next to strangers and, unfortunately, this communal living was to be the norm for the foreseeable future.

We were all extremely happy that the war was over. It's easy to take life for granted, but living through years of sheer terror gave us an indescribable appreciation for living in peace. But as wonderful as it was to experience this new existence, our post-war life took on a monotonous daily grind. Once we had stood in line for food, most of us stayed at the police station while Mother and Karl-Heinz stood in another line to apply for more permanent housing. While both our house and our grandparents' house were gone, the land where they stood was still ours legally, but sorting all that out would take an indeterminable amount of time. Not only was the government in disarray, but the city itself would take years to rebuild. It was questionable if we could even see the land we owned beneath the piles of stone and brick. For now, we had no choice but to be dependent on what was given to us. But, after several days of answering questions and speaking to officials, Mother only knew we had to wait until adequate housing was found for our large family.

In the meantime, there was no place for any of us to play outside; there was simply too much damage. Until heavy machinery was brought in, walking around the police station was hazardous with broken glass, twisted metal, brick, nails, and shell holes everywhere. In addition to the potential for injury, Mother was also worried about strangers around every corner. As protective as ever, she still required us to hold hands when we walked to get food and returned to our second story home over the police station. Not only were we surrounded by Bremen residents we didn't know, but we were also surrounded by returning soldiers and plenty of foreigners. Basically, everywhere we looked there were strangers in the streets and Mother was too accustomed to being wary of people she didn't know to start trusting them now.

Both British and American military occupied Bremen, but it was the Americans we saw the most. Just as my first exposure to them had been during our recent border crossing into the west, I found them exuberant, loud, and bold. Most were certainly friendly and their good nature was infectious, but for a family who never hugged or said we loved one another, we found them a little intimidating and heeded Mother's caution to keep our distance. And that wasn't easy. Many of the servicemen were armed with chocolate bars and liberally handed them out to young German children. My mouth watered at the thought of the delicacy that I had gone without for so long, but I feared my mother's wrath more than I wanted that chocolate, so I never accepted the gift.

We were left with few diversions during the day but to humor ourselves in our little section of the upper floor. Our only true breaths of fresh air were during our excursions to and from the chow lines at each meal. We were one of several large families that had been assigned bunks above the police station, so there was no privacy any time of the day or night. We were, therefore, very excited two months later when we heard we would be moving to a vacant military barracks.

I thought back to the move from Bremen to Krumhermsdorf and compared it with this move. They could not have been more different. In 1943, we had packed our belongings for days and furniture movers worked tirelessly to see that our furniture was sent by train to the east before we arrived. *This* move was considerably less work—we just left the police station from the city center and walked two miles down the road to the barracks. No pesky possessions to pack or furniture to ship ahead. But despite the lack of material goods to carry to our new "home," we were all excited to begin again elsewhere.

Manpower and machinery along with single individuals using their own shovels and hands were beginning to make a difference in the damage to the city. Everywhere we walked there were two things most prevalent: first, streets were slowly being cleared and second, there was so much more work to do before the city was whole again. I was pleased to see the city center was mostly intact and the statue of Roland still stood gazing at us as we walked by. But after passing the statue, I was shaken to realize my father's favorite pastry shop was gutted by fire, its windows gone and the quaint interior a blackened shell. I wondered what had happened to the sweet, elderly shopkeeper who always greeted us when we bought his baked goods, but knew no one to ask.

When we arrived at the wooden barracks, we were met by an official at the entrance in front of double doors. He ushered us into the structure where a long hallway stretched the length of the building. There were rooms off either side of the hallway with one family per room, but because our family was so large, we were assigned two rooms. With the exception of a small coal stove, the rooms were totally unfurnished. As with the police station, we were provided with straw for "bedding," but Mother was happy. We might have to sleep on the floor with straw for mattresses, but in time she knew we could collect what we needed. That coal stove would give us the ability to cook meals and take hot baths, and we were in desperate need of both.

Over the next few months, life settled into a new normal. Enough land had been cleaned of debris around the barracks that we could eventually go outside to play. Even then, Mother still insisted we be supervised while outside. So if she was busy inside, she would ask Helga or Elfriede to watch us. I suppose knowing Frau Meier had lost one of her two children was enough to reinforce Mother's strict rules about staying together, even though the war was over.

We were provided ration cards again and could stand in line (we were now professionals in the art) for a half pound of flour, butter, and other staples. The rations were provided at set times each week, so Mother made sure she and one or two of us were there in line to ensure we didn't miss that appointment time. Helga and Elfriede had somehow found an opportunity to befriend a couple of American servicemen and, while Mother frowned on the association, the two men proved beneficial to the family when they hauled a small round, tin tub into one of the rooms for our use. It probably came from one of the bombed out houses in Bremen, but we knew we had to make do with what we found.

I'd like to say that first bath was heavenly, but the truth was… it was disgusting! As before, we all had to share the same tub and the same water, but circumstances dictated that the water be changed more often since we were entirely too dirty to leave the water anything but filthy. We couldn't keep the water warm enough, so the first bath was a cold affair, but one that was effective in cutting through months of dirt and grime. Before we each washed our hair, Mother used a pair of scissors borrowed from a family down the hall to cut our hair to a more manageable length. After I had my turn at washing my tangled hair and it air-dried, it felt incredibly lighter.

In time, a few donations from organizations and individuals were brought to us. And a "new" wardrobe was a luxury. I think Mother probably burned all our old clothes. After all, I'm sure those clothes would not have survived a good scrubbing like the ones our bodies had to endure. The threads were so caked with dried mud, they were brittle, but they had certainly served their purpose. The first collections of clothes and shoes we received from some unnamed charity were not only ill-fitting, but had been handed down for some time. Yet compared to what we had been wearing the past few months, the fabric felt like high quality silk or satin against my skin, and my "new" shoes were soft and supple against my blistered feet.

The military barracks we now called home was a long wooden one-level structure not far from a major road. Traffic was heavy in front of the barracks with Allied vehicles running up and down the road, particularly during the day. Foot traffic was busy as well and since both our windows faced the street, we had a front row seat to all the hum of activity in rebuilding Bremen. But, one day after Mother was frightened by an Allied serviceman peering in one of our windows, she managed to find some bed sheets and promptly used them as curtains for the windows in both our living quarters.

Perhaps six months after returning to Bremen, Mother returned from another round of talks with the Red Cross with Frau Meier about our missing family members. When she walked back through our door, I could tell she finally had news. I could also tell it wasn't good.

"What's wrong, Mutti?" I asked as she made her way to a small wooden chair Karl-Heinz had found nearby.

Helga and Elfriede realized Mother had important information to share with us and gathered our younger siblings as quickly as possible. We sat cross-legged on the floor in a semi-circle facing our mother, our eyes wide with anticipation.

"Have you heard anything about Erich Meier?" Helga asked hopefully.

"No." Mother sat in the chair dejectedly, her hands limp in her lap. "There is no word about Erich and none on your brother Günter either."

"What about Vati? Did you learn something about our father?" Karl-Heinz asked quietly.

Realizing she was scaring us, Mother looked around and smiled to reassure us. "I don't yet know everything about Diedrich, but I did learn a little today." She took a deep breath and began again, "You all know your father was sent to the Eastern Front last autumn. Well, the Red Cross has information that your father was captured by the Soviets just before the war ended."

"Is he... alive?" I asked tearfully, the pain almost hard to fathom.

"I don't know," Mother answered truthfully. "But we can pray that if he's still a prisoner of war that he will continue to be safe."

We all nodded, shedding tears and sniffling while Egon openly cried for the father he was too young to really know. What I wouldn't really comprehend for years to come is how very guilty my mother felt about my father's situation. She was convinced his adultery in Berlin, followed by her informing his superiors of his actions, led directly to his being sent to the Eastern Front. His eventual capture by the Soviets was, in her estimation, all her fault and she carried that guilt quietly but deeply within her.

Saying we had no possessions during that period was not exactly accurate. Certainly we had each other, but we did have two separate parcels of possessions that were important to us. Mother's quick thinking in Saxony to sew our identification inside the lining of her jacket had proven a lifesaver over and over again. With it, we had gained access from Soviet-occupied east Germany into west Germany, and it had legitimized our claim to housing and aid now that we were in Bremen. I'm not sure where we would have been without it.

But the other items Mother had thought to place in her jacket lining were a small collection of family photographs. Few and seemingly insignificant, as an adult I have been forever grateful to my mother for rescuing those pictures and preserving them for posterity. The only other family I had ever known had been killed during the war, their homes and belongings destroyed with them. Had Mother's sense of sentimentality not complemented her practical side, I would not have had those treasures from my childhood to look back at now. And those same photos were our main items of décor pinned to the walls in those military barracks in 1945. I would stare at them endlessly, memorizing every face, every feature. I knew them intimately then; I still do today.

Christmas 1945 was one of the most bittersweet holidays I ever remembered. Frau Meier and Hans joined our family in the barracks and, though three of our number were missing, we put on smiles and were thankful we were home and healthy. Helga had asked if she could invite one of the American servicemen she had befriended to our little get-together and, though Mother had scolded her soundly about foreigners and strangers, the GI made a quick appearance to drop off gifts to us all—chocolate candy and gum. As our eyes widened over the treat, Mother thanked him sheepishly. He grinned at Mother, winked at Helga, and waved at the rest of us before leaving to rousing applause! For once, I was grateful my sister was such a flirt.

Mother had prepared hot apple cider, Frau Meier had baked sugar cookies, and now we had chocolate. There were no other presents, but we felt rich, and the food and drink certainly made the mood much more festive than I would have thought possible. We celebrated by singing carols around the picture of a tree Waltraut and Inge had drawn, and grew sleepy listening to Mother and Frau Meier talking about Christmases past. Reminiscing was perilous to the good mood that had prevailed throughout the evening and inevitably ended with the two mothers misty-eyed.

It had been just over a year since Frau Meier had heard from her husband. The Luftwaffe pilot had been sent to the Ardennes Forest in an offensive the Allied forces called "The Battle of the Bulge." And within the past week she had just learned her husband was officially classified as missing in action. By now, we had all seen men who returned from war, looking fatigued and broken, walking into the city to find their families, but our mothers were realists. The more time that passed, the less likely their husbands would ever return. And as for their missing sons, there was still no word as to what had happened to Erich and Günter. It was debatable which was more torturous—some knowledge or none at all.

Throughout the coming year we did little but exist. There was no paid work for the masses and our family had no choice but to rely on any assistance we could receive. Rations for foods, handouts for clothes, recovered throw-aways for furniture. Our tandem rooms in the barracks looked like a hodge podge designed by a mad decorator, but it was functional and that's all that mattered.

Little by little, progress was being made clearing debris. Our former school was fortunate to have sustained minimal damage during earlier air raids, so it didn't take long for the building to be repaired and deemed safe. For the first time in years, I was able to attend classes on a part-time basis and I was glad to have some solid structure back to my days. But, attending school felt decidedly different than before the war. It was difficult for our teachers to determine what grade any of us should be in, since we had attended school so sporadically during the war, so classes began by simply reviewing material we had long forgotten.

And we were not just children attempting to recapture a lost education—we were children who had lost the innocence of youth. Many desks sat empty, and the implications behind each empty desk was inescapable. Each of us, teachers and students alike, had been affected by the war, and we all had friends or family missing, dead, or both. Being intimately familiar with death tempered our delight in being able to play outside again and it haunted us in memories of those no longer beside us.

School was not the same without Günter leading the way up the stairs, catching all the girls' eyes, and charming all the teachers; Manfred and Uta weren't there to race us down the street to the school building, and so many other friends were missing that our class sizes were much smaller. There were few teachers I recognized, and I found myself trying not to think about where all my former teachers and classmates were. Hans Meier went to a different school, but at least the children living in other rooms in our barracks/home were now attending our school. It was a new beginning, but the halls echoed with the stilled voices of those who were not there and who we feared would never come back.

By mid-1947, the military barracks had become home to us. We had come to think of our two rooms as our "apartment" with "neighbors" in adjoining "apartments." Most of the same people had been living in the barracks next to us for almost two years, so we had become good friends. Granted, we were all a little cramped, but part of the beauty of not owning much was that we didn't need nearly as much room.

Rather than standing in extremely long lines now, we had set times we went for groceries with our ration cards once a week. We still had to wait, but the time we did so was much shorter because the process was now much better organized. We were, however, expected to be there during our appointed time or else we forfeited our time slot and had to wait until our next scheduled visit.

"Edith, why don't you and Karl-Heinz come with me this morning?" Mother motioned to us while she gathered our ration cards.

Leaving Helga and Elfriede to do my chores, I jumped up and grabbed my coat, eager to get out of the barracks into the bright morning sun. Karl-Heinz was close behind me.

"Are you both ready?" Mother asked as she grabbed a sweater. "It may be a little cool outside, Karl-Heinz. You may want to take a coat."

Karl-Heinz, who had just turned fourteen, hesitated and then decided to take her advice. After shrugging into his coat, he opened the door to the hallway and the three of us walked toward the double doors.

"I think Helga really likes that new American soldier," I told Mother as we stepped through the barrack's entrance.

"We've lived here for two years and I've noticed throughout that entire time that Helga has liked every American soldier." Karl-Heinz snickered as he bounced from the entrance onto the street.

Mother laughed heartily. "She's almost seventeen. That's what seventeen-year-old girls do."

"Act silly?" I asked half-seriously.

"No." Mother laughed a little harder. "Flirt."

"I think Edith was right. She just acts silly," Karl-Heinz chimed in as we turned left in front of the barracks and headed for the food line.

We all laughed until our sides hurt, but Mother suddenly stopped in her tracks, stunned, and turned to look back toward the barracks.

"Dirk?"

An extremely thin, stooped man wearing a tattered German Army uniform and coat had just passed us in the street, but at her call he slowly turned around. I didn't recognize him, but somehow my mother had.

My father had come home.

FOURTEEN
LOOSE ENDS

"Marta." My father's voice was hoarse with emotion as his eyes met hers. And then I saw something I had never seen before. My father embraced my mother with both arms in a bone-numbing bear hug, burying his face in her shoulder. They stood together for a long time, swaying slightly as they each cried unashamedly.

My father was forty-eight years old, but he appeared much older and he looked so different, so thin, weathered, beaten down. The war had ended two years ago, yet here was this ghost from our past standing in front of us. He was still wearing his Army uniform and coat, even though both had certainly seen better days, and he had lost so much weight that both were ill-fitting. My father had just walked passed us in the street, not an arm's length away, and Karl-Heinz and I hadn't even known it was him. But something in his gait, his build had caught Mother's attention and she had known instinctively that the husband she had privately given up for dead was home. It was a staggering surprise.

Initially, Karl-Heinz and I were speechless as we watched them hug. But their mournful weeping at his unexpected arrival affected us both deeply and I didn't even realize I was crying until I felt the tears flowing down my cheeks. My heart was bursting. I had prayed so long for this moment and now that it was upon me, I could hardly believe it was actually happening. I was sure that I would wake up any moment and find that this was a dream. After several minutes, our father turned our way and gathered us to him in each arm as we all cried like babies in the middle of the street.

"Vati." I sobbed his name and squeezed him as hard as I could.

"Edith," Father managed to say, "you've grown so much, and Karl-Heinz, I can't believe you are so tall."

Wrapping her arms around us all, Mother encouraged us to return to the military barracks we called home. "The rest of your children will be just as happy to see you, Dirk."

He nodded and we all walked back to the apartment, our arms locked together as we did so, afraid to let go lest one of us evaporate into thin air. We opened the double doors of the barracks, walked down the hall and just before we reached the first of our two rooms, Karl-Heinz ran ahead and opened the door wide without saying a word to our siblings. The look on their faces was laughable. They were as astonished as Karl-Heinz and I had been and just as much at a loss for words. For just a moment in time, Helga and Elfriede seemed perfectly frozen in mid-action, unable to move or to speak. But then the dam burst and they both ran to greet Father.

"Vati!" Helga's voice was raspy with feeling as she faced him, standing close enough to study his features intently. "Vati, is it really you?"

Father could barely answer. He simply nodded and managed a quiet, "Yes. It is good to be home."

As if they had finally been given permission, my two oldest sisters embraced our father and the Röpke reunion began anew. We all stood around him, laughing, crying, not quite believing our eyes, and then I noticed that my younger siblings were a little more reticent in joining in the boisterous homecoming celebrations.

Father noticed as well and bent down on one knee, offering his outstretched arms to Waltraut, Inge, and Egon. The younger girls, now nine and seven years old respectively, smiled and made their way to him shyly, but Egon continued to hold back. Father hugged the two girls, soaking in the sight of them and then finally crooked his index finger and winked, beckoning six-year-old Egon.

"Can this young man be my youngest child?" Father asked as he admired Egon, and my brother grinned as Father ruffled his hair and hugged him roughly.

Noting again how very fragile he appeared, Mother insisted he sit down while giving us all orders to get him food and drink. He accepted water and drank rapidly, draining the glass in no time. She offered him a cool, wet towel and he scrubbed his face and the back of his neck with closed eyes, savoring the feel of the dampness against his skin. I was not surprised at the dirt left behind on that towel—I had seen the same result when I finally had my first bath after escaping the east two years before. I knew how much better he would feel once he had bathed and rested.

"Where is Günter?" he said, looking around, realizing their oldest son was not in the room.

Mother swallowed, dreading the look on Father's face when she told him what little she had learned. "I don't know. I've been to the Red Cross often for any updates on his whereabouts, but so far there has been no word. At least where you were concerned I had finally received news you had been captured on the Eastern Front. I didn't know anything more than that about you, and I know nothing at all about Günter."

Father gritted his teeth, not wanting to display his emotions openly to us on hearing that Günter was not with us. "We will work together to find him, Marta."

Mother told Helga to ask one of the neighbors if we could borrow some men's bed clothes. While she asked Elfriede to heat some water on the stove, she directed Karl-Heinz to get the tub ready. Ushering the rest of us into another room, she and Karl-Heinz helped Father to his feet and out of his threadbare uniform. Once the tub was filled, they lowered Father into the warm water while Mother helped him bathe. I'm not sure how long Father stayed in that tub and soaked, but when he was out and dressed, he was led immediately to Mother's bed where he fell into a deep sleep.

Father slept long into the next day and left his bed only to eat and make his way to the bathroom. Mother asked us all to be as quiet as possible whenever we were in the house, and it was a request we honored easily, both from respect for our father and a fearful awe of what he had endured during his absence from us. There were so many burning questions on our tongues: "Where were you taken as prisoner? What happened there? Did you escape?" Each day we hoped he was stronger and would feel more like talking to quench our insatiable thirst for answers—answers to questions we had waited two long years to ask, but he had lived two long years to forget.

It was obvious he was beyond tired, but after several days he was finally able to sit with us in the living room for longer blocks of time. And while he would never openly share all the details of his ordeal, I suppose he knew we deserved to at least know the most important facts. I remember him closing his eyes briefly one day, settling back in the chair in which he was sitting, willing to give us a glimpse into the hell he had survived.

Captured by the Soviets on the Eastern Front in late '44, he was transported to a prisoner of war camp somewhere in the Soviet Union. He was never completely sure why he was finally released, but assumed it was because of good behavior or his waning health, or both. What little I learned about his personal experience during captivity, I learned in quick, quiet comments of reflection over many years: food was rationed to all prisoners and there was no medical treatment to speak of. The weather was bitterly cold and they were required to do heavy labor outdoors for hours every day. I recall him saying years later that he had shoveled a lot of snow while in the Soviet Union.

I read later that there were more than 3.5 million German soldiers held prisoner in the Soviet Union by the time World War II was over. The Soviet gulags were forced labor camps that incorporated POWs into Stalin's workforce under provisions of the Yalta Agreement. Daily food rations at some prisons included a little black bread, spaghetti, some meat, sugar, vegetables, and rice. But, the grueling manual labor for long hours outdoors in the most extreme weather conditions took its toll. By 1952, approximately 1 million German POWs died in the camps and another 1.5 million are still listed as missing in action. Of an estimated 875,000 German civilians kidnapped and sent to the camps, half of those died. Reading those statistics was chilling. Two years in a gulag had seemed an indescribable length of time, but I know now that we were fortunate to be reunited with our father in 1947, since the last German POWs weren't released from the USSR until 1955.

Frau Meier came by to meet Father within the first week of his return, and she and Hans visited often in the months and years to come. And while she celebrated alongside my mother, she was not as fortunate concerning her own husband, who had been listed as missing in action and was now presumed dead. Even though 1947 was slowly disappearing, she continued to hold out hope, but was also realistic enough to know that a good outcome was highly unlikely. Since her oldest son, Erich, had not been in the service, there was no such list to review, no real means of knowing where he might be, what might have happened to him. He had been lost in a crowd during our walk westward; he had simply vanished. Even though there was no definitive word on her husband, conclusions could be drawn on him, but with her son, the not-knowing, the gnawing need-to-know seemed to disturb her the most. The common bond between Frau Meier and my mother remained strong, but their common worries were changing. Mother's husband had returned and she now had him to lean on and to support her in the search for their oldest son.

About a week after coming home, my parents went together to the Red Cross to see if there had been any word on Günter. Mother had been checking with officials several times a month since returning to Bremen, but *this* time when Father and Mother returned home, they finally had an update to share with us.

"Günter was taken captive in the last weeks of the war by Allied troops," Mother told us all shakily.

Helga was as stunned as the rest of us. "But, it has been two years since the war ended. Does the Red Cross know where he is?"

Mother was unable to utter another word and simply looked up at Father to provide the answer. "Yes," he said as he glanced at each of us. "Your brother is in Belgium."

"Belgium?" Elfriede leaned against a wall, absorbing the information. "Well, that's not far away. When will he be home?"

Again, Mother was unable to speak, but Father cleared his throat, whether from emotion or in dread I couldn't decide. "Belgium needed manpower to help rebuild their economy and the Allies agreed to send German POWs to camps in Belgium to work."

"Günter is a POW in Belgium." Helga breathed. "Where, Vati?"

"Apparently, he's working in a coal mine," Father answered. "I don't know when he'll be allowed to come home."

Mother stiffened and looked at all of us with determination. "But at last we know that Günter is alive and we know where he is. We will just have to keep checking in with the Red Cross and hope we learn more as time goes by."

Just as it had been with Father, it was good to finally know my oldest brother was alive, but until he was actually back with us, there was no guarantee he would survive the ordeal he was going through. I would feel much better if we were all together again and until that happened, there was an emptiness in my heart as I faced each new day. The irony of Günter working in a coal mine did not escape any of us. Even though Günter was just months away from being eighteen, he had always been quite the ladies' man, immaculate in his dress and his appearance. Besides the long, back-breaking hours he must now be facing in a coal mine, the dirt and grime must be strongly affecting his very pride as well.

At least Father was back with us now. Of course, we had lived for years without him in our household, so it was an adjustment having him back. Though he rarely talked about his experiences as a POW, I could tell it had changed him. His physical condition was certainly worse and he was sick more often than he had been before the war. Not only was he thinner, he walked a little more bent over, moved a little slower. Two years of stress and hard labor in the harsh Russian winters had taken their toll on his middle-aged body. He had aches and pains in his joints that plagued him the rest of his life.

His mental state was different as well. He drank before the war, but he was a drunk afterward. He didn't stay home to drink, but went out to the few bars that had reopened around Bremen. There were nights he didn't come home until the wee hours of the morning. It was a vice that would make for a self-imposed separation from his family at times, affect decisions he would make for years to come, and inevitably shorten his life. And, though he was happy to be home, worries about supporting his family in a country that had been brought to its knees weighed on him heavily.

No one knew how long it would take the economy to rebound, but slowly, streets were cleared and shops were re-opened. After several weeks of resting and consuming a better diet, Father regained much of his strength and joined the ranks of the somewhat-gainfully employed by putting his carpentry skills to good use. He began by taking inventory of our sparsely furnished "apartments" and deciding to do something about it. With the loan of rudimentary tools and found wood, he began assembling a small table and a set of storage shelves for our family's use. Soon he was being "contracted" by our neighbors to build a headboard, a cabinet, or a crib.

Gradually his income became more substantial when he was asked to build furniture for the American GIs and their families stationed in Bremen. Through word of mouth, Father's custom carpentry skills were in high demand and it wasn't long before he was able to earn a modest living. The Americans were not only willing to pay well for his handmade furniture, they even tipped him a little from to time, so much so that he was even able to save a little money each month. A few months later, his meager savings got a bigger boost.

The lots where our house and my grandparents' house once stood were now cleared of debris, but rebuilding a house on either was simply not possible. There wasn't enough raw materials in the country for us to do so, and it would certainly have been cost prohibitive for the materials and labor even if either had been available. Instead, the German government bought both lots from us. Combining the money from the land and the small savings he had accumulated, Father and Mother decided to buy another of the military barracks for our family's sole use.

Almost identical to the barracks we had been living in since our return to Bremen in mid-1945 (and just across the street), our new "house" was a long wooden structure with multiple rooms. Originally built for German troops, Americans GIs had most recently been housed there. Now vacant, it seemed extravagant to have the entire structure to ourselves. No longer would we have just two rooms for our entire family and, most importantly, no longer would we have to stand in line with multiples families to use a communal bathroom. Instead, our parents converted the use of the front rooms to our living, kitchen, and bedrooms, and the back quarters contained our Father's furniture business.

More rooms meant more space and more elbow room. It also meant more windows and, unfortunately, that meant trouble.

Though Father had always been strict, he was more so now. Before the war, he had always been the disciplinarian in our family, but after the war, Helga and Elfriede seemed to receive the brunt of his disciplinary decisions most often. It didn't help that they were at an age—Helga was seventeen and Elfriede sixteen—where they were more love-struck than ever before with every boy who caught their eyes. It also didn't help that there with so many foreign soldiers in Bremen. The Americans in particular were simply an exciting distraction my sisters could simply not resist. And Father had a full-time job trying to rein in the mutual admiration society between a few of the young soldiers living nearby and his two oldest daughters.

One night, after our parents were asleep, Helga and Elfriede quietly slipped out of one of those many windows in our new house to meet up with their newest "boyfriends." It hadn't been their first escape from our parents' watchful eyes, but the two girls had overestimated the time of their return and underestimated the noise they made as they attempted to sneak back into our house on this particular evening.

As they were slipping back in on tiptoe, Father met them at the door, belt in hand, and uttered a word in a tone not used in six years, "Hel-*gaaaa!*"

It was not a pleasant homecoming. Helga had always been in trouble with Father before the war, so Elfriede should have known better than to follow Helga's lead. They paid a high price that night for their poor decisions and it was several days before either of them could sit comfortably. They learned the hard way that Father was a rougher man now due to his time as a POW. But despite the harsher man he was, we all knew that behind that strict disciplinarian was a father who just wanted his children to do what was right. He was a hard man, but he was still my father and I loved him.

Throughout the rest of 1947, there were no other updates on Günter; but by the next spring, we received news that gave us a glimmer of hope. Prisoners from Belgium had been allowed to return home for the past few months, and an agreement had been reached stating that all remaining German POWs would be released by June 1948.

Months passed and we heard nothing. Mother feared the worst—she would never see her oldest son again. She tried not to let her concern consume her days, but I knew it was difficult. It became evident when I walked in our kitchen one morning a few days before Christmas and caught her crying.

"Mutti, what is wrong?" I asked quietly, fearful of alerting the rest of my siblings who were busy eating breakfast around another of father's large, handcrafted tables.

She quickly wiped her eyes with the cuff of her sleeve, attempting to hide the evidence of her sadness.

"Nothing, Edith. I was just thinking about something."

"You were thinking about Günter." I sat my empty milk glass on the kitchen counter and dared her to deny it. "You don't have to pretend you weren't, Mutti. We all miss him and hope he'll be with us soon."

Mother's eyes glistened with unshed tears as she turned to look at me. "You are a very astute young lady, Edith."

I smiled, attempting to lighten her mood. "Well, I will be thirteen in a few more months."

"Yes." Mother crossed her arms and stared at me intently, smiling broadly. "And you've had no childhood. You've had to grow up too quickly."

"We all had to," I said, scuffing the toe of my shoe against the stove's iron feet. "Mutti, I don't really understand what good this war did. I only saw death and destruction and families torn apart, and for what?"

Mother wiped her hands on her apron and turned to stare out the kitchen window. "I don't know, Edith. It's very easy for powerful men to have grand ideas, but the common people are the main ones that suffer for their scheming, and all we want to do is live our lives and do it in peace."

"I'm so glad it's over," I said. "Sometimes, I'm afraid I'll wake up and one of us will be missing—just like Erich Meier or Uta and Manfred. Or… worse…."

"I know." Mother sighed heavily, glancing back at the table surrounded by all her children but one. "God was looking after us."

"And he'll look after Günter, too," I reminded her.

"I know He will," she said softly. "I just pray His Will is to let Günter return to us."

Father entered the kitchen from his shop, taking his coat from the coat rack near the front entrance. He did not miss the sadness in Mother's eyes. "Marta, I have an appointment in the city center. Why don't you go with me? It will do you good."

She patted me on the shoulder, ending our private conversation and loosened the knot on the apron she had been wearing. Father helped her into her coat and turned to face us. "Your mother and I will be back. Karl-Heinz, you are in charge while we are gone."

"What about me?" Helga sat up straight in her chair, indignant. "I'm the oldest one here. I can take care of things while you are out."

"Yes," Father drawled as he looked at her intently. "I know you can do many things while we are out, Helga. That's why I asked Karl-Heinz to be in charge."

Karl-Heinz smiled broadly while Elfriede and I giggled, Helga crossed her arms in a huff, and Father reminded everyone to be on our best behavior while they were away from home.

"I have to do some work in the furniture shop," Karl-Heinz announced with an air of importance. He began walking down the hall toward the business, but turned to face his older sisters still sitting around the table with our younger siblings finishing the morning meal. "I think the rest of you should clean up the house from breakfast while Mutti and Vati are gone."

"*What?*" Helga exploded as Karl-Heinz left the room, which only prompted the rest of us to laugh more. "I will *not* take orders from my younger brother! No wonder he shared a birthday with the Führer—they were both ridiculous leaders!"

"Oh, Helga." Elfriede stood from the table and attempted to stop laughing long enough to reason with her. "Let's just keep the peace. The last thing I want to do is have something go wrong and face an unhappy father."

Helga stood up, fists on her hips, and faced Elfriede. "You mean, you're going to take Karl-Heinz's side over mine?"

Elfriede stood quietly for a moment, deep in thought, before nodding. "Yes, I am. I've found that being on your side only gets me in more trouble with Vati."

"I'll wash the dishes." I went to the kitchen for water.

"I'll sweep the floor." Elfriede grabbed the broom.

Waltraut and Inge began taking the dirty dishes from the table, while Egon sat at the table somberly staring up at Helga.

Helga turned to look down on our baby brother, still eager for a fight. "Well, munchkin, I suppose you're going to jump up and start cleaning, *too?*"

Egon continued to look up at her, his plate half-full of his uneaten breakfast. "No."

At a momentary loss for words, Helga finally grinned from ear to ear.

"Well." She smiled smugly, anxious to claim any victory—no matter how slight. "Did you all hear that? Egon is standing with me. He refuses to listen to Karl-Heinz. Tell them, Egon. Tell them why you didn't start running around the house to clean up."

"Because I'm not finished eating!" Stabbing the last bite of ham with his fork, he stuffed it into his mouth. And with that, Egon hopped from his chair, his empty plate in hand, and helped the rest of us tidy the kitchen.

We all laughed all over again as Helga realized Egon was not going to stand firm with her against Karl-Heinz's "orders." Reluctantly, she surrendered with a long sigh and helped dry the clean plates and utensils.

As soon as our chores were finished, we left the house to play in a small grassy area beside the house that had become our yard. We entertained ourselves with jumping rope, playing tag and running around with no particular destination in mind. It felt great to laugh and play and do so without fear of sirens blaring at any moment. But after an hour or so, the cold winter day drove us back inside. Our noses were red and our fingers felt numb as the heat from the stove seeped through our clothing. As we unraveled from our coats, scarves, and gloves, the front door opened and Mother and Father stepped through, a strange smile spread across each of their faces.

"You look funny, Vati." Inge giggled as we all puzzled over their odd expressions.

"Well, children, your mother and I have a surprise for you," he said as he and Mother stepped farther into our living room.

"A Christmas gift?" Inge cooed excitedly.

"Yes," Mother said. "A Christmas gift."

A tall, thin man with extremely dark skin walked into the room and stood with his hat in his hand, nervously twisting it round and round. His clothes and boots were shabby and his pants were held up with nothing more than a thin length of worn rope. Another young man followed behind the first, shorter, but just as dark-skinned. As their eyes darted around the room, neither man spoke and, based on how malnourished they both looked, I was sure they must be trying to scope the room for any scraps of food lying about.

By now, all the girls in my family had joined Egon in a speechless perusal of the two men who had obviously been invited home by our parents. There were so many displaced Germans wandering through Bremen that it wasn't unusual for strangers to periodically be asked to our house for a hot meal. But, Mother and Father were normally keen on making introductions upon guests' first arrival. On this day, they both stood by mutely in a corner, making me wonder if I should be afraid of these two visitors.

That's when the first man turned and looked at me directly, and I noticed something I had not seen before. Behind the dark skin and features of the man's face peered a pair of brilliant blue eyes that suddenly transported me back in time.

"Günter!" I shrieked and ran into his arms.

Karl-Heinz heard the commotion and came running from the furniture shop down the hall, joining us as we gathered around our oldest brother. We were laughing and crying, unsure which emotion would actually win out. Everyone talked at once, anxious to know how he was, if he was hungry, how he felt. Mother's eyes were shining and her familiar laughter washed over us all, completing the jubilant homecoming.

"Did you know Günter was coming home, Vati?" Karl-Heinz asked, swallowing hard in an attempt to appear less emotional than his sisters.

"I received a telegram last week that said he should arrive today by bus, but I kept it from you all just in case he was delayed longer," Father answered.

Working underground in a coal mine for three years had taken its toll on my brother's complexion. He was older, skinnier, and certainly more earthy-looking than he had been years before, but I was thrilled to have him home again and marveled at how his blue eyes were still as vivid as ever. I firmly believed he was as handsome as he had always been, despite the borrowed clothes he was wearing. "I would have known you anywhere, Günter."

"And I, you, Edith." Günter pinched my nose.

The young man who had shadowed my oldest brother stood quietly nearby. I assumed he was about Günter's age and, because his skin was the same shade as my brother's, I was sure they had served time together in the same camp in Belgium. Of course, an eligible bachelor could not stay hidden for long from Helga, who was eyeing him with interest.

"And you have not introduced your friend, Günter," Helga said with a decidedly sweeter tone than the one she had used earlier in the morning with Karl-Heinz.

"I'm sorry—I forgot. This is my good friend, Alfred Beck." Günter stepped to one side while Alfred swept his hat from his head and bowed slightly in greeting. "I've already spoken to Vati and Mutti and they have agreed that Alfred can live with us for the time being."

"Alfred was in Belgium with Günter. He was born in the east, but since that's under Soviet control, his family won't be allowed here and he can't go back there," Vati said.

Mother led the two young men to chairs and motioned for them to sit. "We have two rooms at the other end of the house we only use for storage. Those can easily be converted to bedrooms for each of you."

My father readily agreed. "And you can both help me in the furniture shop for now."

"*Danke*, Herr Röpke," Alfred said, bowing his head, overcome.

As my siblings plopped on the floor peppering Günter with endless questions and Helga demurely pulled up a chair close to Alfred Beck, I walked to a corner of the room and sat down. I knew instinctively I wanted to remember this moment in time. I knew I wanted to drink it in and be able to recall it as I grew older, to pull it up in my mind during quiet moments of reflection.

It was quite a Christmas gift. My stern father, long-forgiven for his "indiscretion" in Berlin, patted my mother's hand absently before taking a seat himself, showing a rare glimpse into an emotional side I thought had died years ago. But, it was a room filled with emotion. One voice boisterously competed with another in a loud confusion of excited conversation and laughter that echoed through the room. Everyone encircled Günter and Alfred, eager to hear and be heard. Everyone but Mother.

Smiling brightly, Mother quietly took the boys' hats and placed them on hooks near the door. She went to the kitchen, poured two glasses of water, and returned to the room, handing one to her oldest son and the other to his friend. They were so engrossed in their lively discussion, they barely even noticed. Returning to the kitchen, I heard the rustling of cabinet doors, the clatter of utensils, and her light footsteps pacing from one activity to another. She re-entered the room a few moments later with two plates laden with hearty sandwiches and snaked her way through the audience to the two young men. They smiled as she passed them the food and insisted they eat. It did little to slow the rush of words bouncing off the walls.

Mother walked from the inner circle to the edge of the room. She stood, contented, her hands clasped in front of her, and slowly scanned every animated face in that room. And then her eyes met mine and she smiled even more. My heart skipped.

In Grimm's *The Town Musicians of Bremen,* the animals agree they have nothing to lose by leaving their homes—staying only meant death. Instead, they find a new life by working together against incredible odds. Of course, at the end of the fairytale, the animals end their journey before ever making it to Bremen. But that's where the fairytale ends and real life begins. Just as it took years for my entire family to make our way back to Bremen, Grimm's animals finally did as well. In 1953, a bronze statue was erected in Bremen's city center of the donkey, the dog, the cat, and the rooster—one standing atop the other's back—and that image remains an emblem of the city of Bremen.

I smiled back at my mother, leaned against the wall, and inhaled deeply. *Danke, Mutti. Ich liebe dich.*

EPILOGUE

Colonel Pfiffer and his family fled Krumhermsdorf along with others on May 7, 1945. Attempting to reach the closest border, they traveled east, but only made it as far as Saupsdorf before they were forced to return. The Soviets took Colonel Pfiffer into custody and sent him to the Mühlberg Concentration Camp where he died in January 1946.

Frau Meier lived the rest of her life in Bremen. Her husband was presumed killed in action. Her oldest son was never found.

Diedrech Röpke never moved from Bremen. After returning from the Soviet Union two years after the end of WWII, his health continued to decline and was further complicated by alcoholism. He had a heart attack and died at the age of 68 in 1967.

A ladies' man to the end, Günter married twice, but never had children. He died on Christmas Day 1998 in Bremen.

Helga married and had four children. She died of cancer in Hannover in 2000 at the age of 70.

After divorcing her first husband, Elfriede eventually married a US serviceman and moved to the US in 1957. She had four children and died of breast cancer in Texas. She was only 53.

Karl-Heinz and his wife had five children. He trained German Shepherds for the police and learned to be a carpenter like his father. He still lives in Germany near Bremen.

Waltraut married a man from the United States Air Force. They moved to Texas in 1973 and had four children where she continues to reside.

While visiting Elfriede in the US in the 60s, Inge met and married an American and had two sons. She later re-married and passed away in Oklahoma in 2012.

Egon married, had two daughters, and retired from the railroad. He still lives in Germany.

Marta Röpke, who managed to keep her family together through incredible odds, lived the rest of her life in her hometown of Bremen. At the time of this writing, she had 24 grandchildren and 36 great-grandchildren. She lived to be 85.

Edith Röpke met a Texan, Henry "Hank" Harris, who was stationed in Bremerhaven, Germany in the mid-50s. They married, had three daughters (Sylvia, Debbie and Barbara), and traveled the world. They settled in the United States where in 2013, after 55 years of marriage, Hank passed away. Edith still resides in Arkansas and is surrounded by her daughters, six grandchildren and a growing number of great-grandchildren.

Henry "Hank" Harris, United States Air Force, circa 1956. Photo taken around the time Hank was stationed in Bremerhaven, Germany.

The Harris family—L-R: Debbie, Edith, Barbara, Hank and Sylvia. Photo taken in the Philippines where Hank was stationed with the USAF at Clark Air Force Base, 1963.

Edith and Hank Harris. Photo taken in the Philippines, where Hank was stationed with the USAF at Clark Air Force Base, 1963.

Edith Röpke Harris at home in Arkansas holding a picture of her mother, Marta. circa 2003.

Marta on her 85th birthday in Bremen, Germany. Holding a gift from Günter—her favorite food (an eel), weeks before her death in November 1985.

The Harris family—L-R: Debbie, Edith, Sylvia, Hank and Barbara—at Hank's deacon ordination at Mt. Pleasant Baptist Church, Cabot, Arkansas in 2005.

Edith and her daughters celebrate Edith's 80th birthday at a restaurant in Arkansas.
L-R Debbie, Edith, Barbara, and Sylvia. March 2016.

Edith and Cecelia. September 2016.